THE KITH AND KIN OF CAPTAIN JAMES LEEPER AND SUSAN DRAKE, HIS WIFE

By
NELL McNISH GAMBILL

Notice

In many older books, foxing (or discoloration) occurs and, in some instances, print lightens with wear and age. Reprinted books, such as this, often duplicate these flaws, notwithstanding efforts to reduce or eliminate them. The pages of this reprint have been digitally enhanced and, where possible, the flaws eliminated in order to provide clarity of content and a pleasant reading experience.

Copyright, 1946, by Nell McNish Gambill

Reprinted by:

Janaway Publishing, Inc.
732 Kelsey Ct.
Santa Maria, California 93454
(805) 925-1038
www.janawaygenealogy.com

2007, 2012

ISBN: 978-1-59641-113-5

Made in the United States of America

FOREWORD

IN SEARCHING FOR MATERIAL to build this book around the family of Captain James Leeper and Susan Drake, the first couple married in old Fort Nashborough, 1780, and their kith and kin, records were found also of other families allied to other descendants of these early settlers in Nashville, Tennessee, than the writer's posterity, for whom this book was primarily intended. These records have been included.

With the exception of a very few names, the lineage descending from Captain Leeper and his wife is complete. My purpose has been to show the connection between the older members of the families, rather than to carry down each separate line. Bits of history and mention of interesting events are interspersed throughout the genealogical chronicles.

The records in this book have come from near and far, and I wish to offer the grateful thanks I owe to those who have been so good as to help me.

It is to be deplored that the married life of James Leeper and Susan Drake was of such short duration, and that the Leeper surname could not be carried on among his descendants. But through his daughter, Sarah Leeper, who became the wife of Alexander Smith, Captain Leeper's fine traits of character have been transmitted to the latter-day sons and daughters who proudly call him ancestor. Time has written little change in the spirit and courage of these children of Tennessee's pioneer-founders. They still are building, still carrying-on, with the same fine fervor which characterized their forbears in the wilderness. Year after year, the descendants of old Fort Nashborough's dauntless heroes and heroines march on in the achievement of just living—no less splendid a feat and needing no less courage than their ancestors' service to America in bringing civilization to the wild frontier that became Tennessee.

NELL McNISH GAMBILL.

TABLE OF CONTENTS

	PAGE
Foreword	III
PART 1. Ancestry and Kindred of William Wheless Gambill, Descended from Captain James Leeper, and Susan Drake, His Wife	VII
Captain James Leeper, the First Marriage in Old Fort Nashborough, and Notes on the Leeper Family	12
Drake Family	23
Smith and Descended Families	71
Criddle Family	88
Ewing Family	108
Gambill Family	116
Wheless Family	125
PART II. Ancestry and Kindred of Nell McNish Gambill, Wife of William Wheless Gambill	129
McNish Family	131
Dean Family	161
Stump Family	164
Marshall Family	173
PART III. Tennessee Historical Miscellany	179
Tennessee as It Was Soon after the Marriage of Captain James Leeper and Susan Drake	181
The Pioneers of Tennessee	182
The Cumberland Compact	183
On the Banks of the Beautiful Wautauga	184
The Great Seal of the State of Tennessee	185
The State Flower of Tennessee, The Volunteer State	194
Tennessee State Song	194
Nashville's First Postmaster	194
The Author's Epilogue	196

THE KITH AND KIN OF CAPTAIN JAMES LEEPER
AND SUSAN DRAKE, HIS WIFE

Part I
ANCESTRY AND KINDRED OF WILLIAM WHELESS GAMBILL DESCENDED FROM CAPTAIN JAMES LEEPER AND SUSAN DRAKE, HIS WIFE

SARAH LEEPER SMITH
(Daughter of Captain James Leiper & Susan Drake)
Wife of Alexander Smith

The Kith and Kin of Captain James Leeper and Susan Drake, His Wife

Leeper

THE HISTORY OF TENNESSEE began nearly two centuries before the marriage in 1780 of James Leeper and Susan Drake at old Fort Nashborough. Its territory was included in the grant to Sir Walter Raleigh, 1584, and in the grant of Carolina, 1663. It is believed, though not proven, that it was at the site of Memphis that De Soto reached the Mississippi River, and Fort Prud'homme, built in 1682 by La Salle, was probably on the same site.

In 1750, Doctor Thomas Walker led a band of Virginians to the Cumberland River and Mountains, which they named thus in honor of the Duke of Cumberland. In 1756 or 1757, Fort Loudon was built on the Little Tennessee River, as an outpost against the French. This was about thirty miles south of the site of Knoxville, was captured, 1760, by the Cherokees, and its defenders and some near-by settlers were massacred. The land of Tennessee was considered a common hunting ground by several Indian tribes, and part was claimed by right of conquest by the Iroquois of New York. This claim was ceded, 1768, to the English, and the next year settlers' cabins appeared on the Watauga and Holston Rivers. Other hardy spirits, from Virginia and North Carolina, came into the wilderness to found new homes. It was thought that the land belonged to Virginia, but later established that it should be considered part of North Carolina. That Colony, however, took little interest in the settlements, and they took steps, in 1772, to act jointly in self-protection against the Indians. The Watauga Association was formed and assumed the government. This might be considered as the true beginning of Tennessee. Courts were established, land was purchased from the Indians, and the plan was to set up a distinct colony, with a governor to be appointed by the Crown.

The outbreak of the Revolution changed all this, and in 1776 the settlers requested definite connection with the State of North Carolina. The land of Tennessee became Washington District, and, the next year, 1777, Washington County, North Carolina, with the Mississippi for its western boundary. Named for the great General under whose leadership our national independence was won, the spirit of valor and patriotism, from the start of Tennessee's history, was dominant. Under John Sevier and Evan Shelby the mountainmen gave magnificent service to the American cause, one of their most splendid achievements being the victory of King's Mountain.

As the population increased, new counties were formed out of the original Washington. After the War, in 1784, North Carolina made proffer of this, her western territory, to the general government of the United States, but the people of Tennessee resented this and determined to set up their own State. North Carolina repealed the act of cession, but the movement for independence continued, and in 1785 there was organized the "State of Frankland," whose name soon became "Franklin." Sevier was chosen for Governor. Petition was sent to Congress for recognition of the new State, but this was not carried out. North Carolina still claimed the ownership of the land, and, in 1790, again ceded it to the general government, now established under the Constitution. The national Congress accepted the grant and the later Tennessee now became, by Act of May 26, 1790, the "Territory south of the River Ohio." William Blount became Governor, and Knoxville was made the Capital, thus established in 1792.

The Legislature of the Territory, 1795, ordered a census taken of the inhabitants, and this showed that more than sixty thousand free persons lived there. That figure was the one required before Statehood could be granted. A Convention to form a State Constitution met in Knoxville, January 11, 1796, and John Sevier was elected Governor, William Blount and William Cocke being chosen for United States Senators. On June 1, 1796, Tennessee became the sixteenth State of the Union.

In 1843, Nashville became the Capital of Tennessee. This place was the home of Captain James Leeper and Susan Drake, his wife, and of many other families recorded in this book. It was founded in 1780, the year of James Leeper's marriage to Susan Drake. Nashville was called Nashborough until 1784, and was, in its beginnings, a fort—old Fort Nashborough. This "advance guard of western civilization," as it has been described, was set up in the wild frontier country by some two hundred hardy pioneers, led by James Robertson. Among them was Captain James Leeper. It was named in honor either of Abner Nash, then Governor of North

Carolina, or his brother, General Francis Nash, of the Revolution, perhaps to commemorate them both.* Though not until 1843 did Nashville become officially the State Capital, nevertheless, it was the seat of the State Legislature, from 1812, except for the years between 1815 and 1826.

From the gallant little settlement around old Fort Nashborough in 1780 has grown the great modern city of Nashville, one of the industrial centres of the country, concerned in a wide diversity of agricultural, manufacturing, and commercial interests. Not only a metropolis of business, and not only the governmental seat of a great State, Nashville, known as "The Athens of the South," is eminent as one of the foremost educational centres of the United States. Among its best-known institutions of learning and art are Vanderbilt University, Peabody College, Scarritt College, Ward-Belmont College, and Fisk University, this last being for the higher education of Negroes.

Nashville is a place of beauty, as well as culture, with three large parks, and many handsome structures. The citizens are ever striving to make their city even more attractive, and, to this end, the work of many garden-clubs and flower-associations is directed. Through the untiring efforts of the Iris Association, and the climatic conditions favorable to this flower, Nashville is frequently called "The Iris City."

Two Presidents of the United States, Andrew Jackson and James Polk, lived in Nashville. President Jackson's beautiful old homestead, The Hermitage, still stands, and is visited by hundreds of people every year. His and his family's resting-places are in the little cemetery on the grounds of the estate. President Polk's mortal remains lie in the grounds of the State Capitol.

---

*Officially, the commemoration was of General Nash, as evidenced in the grant of Nashville's charter, 1784, by the North Carolina Legislature: "Be it enacted by the General Assembly of the State of North Carolina and it is hereby enacted by the authority of the same that the directors or trustees hereinafter appointed, or a majority of them, shall, so soon as may be after the passing of this act, cause two hundred acres of land situated on the south side of Cumberland river at a place called the Bluff, adjacent to French Lick, in which the said Lick shall not be included, to be laid off in lots of one acre each, with convenient streets, lanes, and alleys, reserving four acres for the purpose of erecting public buildings, on which land, so laid off according to the directions of this act, is hereby constituted, erected, and established a town and shall be called and known by the name of Nash-ville in memory of the patriotic and brave General Nash." Brigadier-General Francis Nash, of Orange County, North Carolina, was killed in the Battle of Germantown, 1777. He was born, about 1742, at Templeton Manor, the homestead of his father, John Nash, in Virginia.

It is a far journey in imagination from Nashville of today, the great, established city of wealth and culture, and little, splendid Fort Nashborough of 1780. Built of rough logs, and with a stockade of them, it stood on the present site of the Telephone Building, at the corner of Third Avenue and Church Street. A bronze tablet on the building reads: "The old fort and stockade of the Robertson Party established here in 1779. First marriage of the settlement celebrated in fort 1780. Capt. James Leiper and Miss Susan Drake. Erected by Exchange Club 1928."

A descendant of Captain Leeper and his wife (his name often spelled "Leiper"), Mrs. W. S. Armistead, read the following account of her ancestor and the beginnings of Nashville at a meeting of the Cumberland Chapter, Daughters of the American Revolution.

"The subject of this sketch lived and died among those stirring times when the colonies were moved by an inspiration for freedom, when they were engaged in the great struggle for independence, and when the hardy and adventurous pioneers were answering the call of the wild, undeveloped country lying between the Mississippi and the mountains forming the natural western boundary of North Carolina and Virginia. Life was then full of action and beset by danger, and the wisest of their day and generation had no vision of the possibilities of the country which they were establishing for themselves and their posterity.

"The country in and about the Cumberland settlement had been explored by Spencer, Demonbreun, and other pioneers and hunters, and it was their reports, reaching the Wautauga settlers, concerning the fertility and attractiveness of the lands along the Cumberland, that inspired the expedition of Robertson and his companions. A small band of these pioneers had arrived as early as the spring of 1779, planted a field of corn, selected a place for their fort, started the work of building, and left it under the protection of a few of their number.

"In 1779 and 1780, the colony arrived, in two sections: one, consisting of men only, traveling by land, under command of Robertson; and the other, men, women, and children, with a few Negro slaves, traveling by water, down the Tennessee and up the Cumberland from the Ohio, under the command of Donelson. Their respective journeys and the dangers and hardships endured are narrated in Ramsey's Annals and other historical works. The journey by water, under Donelson, especially has been fitly characterized as one of the most remarkable achievements of the kind recorded in history.

"Robertson was a man of unusual executive ability and was recognized as the head of the Cumberland settlement. He it was who superintended the construction of the fort and defenses of the new colony, and who introduced military organization and discipline for the protection of this outpost of civilization. Robertson, like all great leaders, was an excellent judge of the qualities and capabilities of men, and it argues no little for the worth and merit of James Leiper that he was selected as one of the Captains in the Regiment which Robertson organized out of the colonists fit for military service.

"The Indians had shown themselves to be quite hostile to the party that made the journey under Donelson. They were constantly excited to hostility through British influence, and were naturally at enmity toward these pioneers, who had intrenched themselves in the very heart of their hunting-ground. Robertson and his Captains knew only too well that the fort, sooner or later, would be the point of attack by the Indians. The arts of peace, however, were not neglected. The settlers built houses and cultivated the soil with their rifles in their hands, so to speak. They explored the country and took up land in what afterwards became Davidson, Sumner, Williamson, Rutherford, and Giles Counties. Leiper's Fork, in Williamson County, takes its name from Captain James Leiper, who entered lands in that vicinity, and also on Richland Creek in Giles County.

"In those perilous days, the arrow of the Indian was not the only menace to the peace of mind of our restless and daring frontiersman. He was not invulnerable to Cupid's dart, and so, in the summer of 1780, although corn was scarce and to be had only at a fabulous price, there was a wedding-feast spread in the fort on the Cumberland, celebrating the nuptials of Miss Susan Drake and Captain James Leiper. The marriage was solemnized by Colonel James B. Robertson, as the authorized officiant. This was the first wedding in the new country, west of the Cumberland Mountains.

"Their dream of long life and happiness here together was destined to an early and cruel awakening. In the spring of 1781, on April 2, several Indians were observed, skulking about the fort. Colonel James Robertson selected twenty men, among the number Captain Leiper, who had established a reputation for bravery and reckless daring, for the purpose of driving off the Indians and to reconnoitre the wooded country and cane-breaks, south of the fort.

"Armed and mounted, Colonel Robertson and his company rode out from the fort, in the direction of a large spring, situated at the foot of what is now Church Street, in Nashville. The fort was situated on the bluff, about where the Court House now stands. The party had not proceeded far when they discovered a large band of Indians, between three and four hundred, in their front. At the same time, another band, of about equal numbers, who had been in hiding, rose up toward the rear and rapidly formed a line intercepting retreat to the fort. Robertson and his men dismounted, tied their horses, and prepared to give battle against such hopeless odds. When the firing began, the horses became frightened and broke away, running in the direction of what is now Capitol Hill. Some of the Indians nearest to the fort were tempted by cupidity, started in pursuit, and captured the horses. This weakened the line cutting off Robertson's party from the fort. Robertson's wife had been watching the progress of events from the lookout at the fort, and, at this juncture, directed that the settlers' dogs, some fifty in number, exceedingly ferocious, and trained to hunt Indians, be turned out through the gate. They made a sudden and savage attack upon the Indians nearest the fort, and, in the confusion, Robertson's band made a dash to reach it. He and twelve others succeeded, but eight of the party met death at the hands of the enemy, among them the gallant Buchanon and brave Captain Leiper. 'Greater love than this hath no man, that a man lay down his life for his friends.'

"The Indians went away, without further effort to molest the fort. Two of them were killed, and a number wounded, but the full extent of their losses was not known. They had captured nineteen of the horses and thus had the means of carrying off their wounded.

"Captain Leiper's body was buried on the hill, now south of the Capitol, and about where the Capitol Annex now stands. Cut down thus untimely, he did not live to see his child, Sarah Jane Leiper, who was born about three months after her father's death. The widow and her infant daughter continued to live in the fort, until the former, some three years later, was accidentally killed by the discharge of a gun, falling from a rack over the door. She was laid to rest beside her husband.

"Little Sarah Jane Leiper was taken and reared by a maternal uncle, either Benjamin or Joseph Drake, who had settled on Whites

Creek, on the north side of the Cumberland and several miles from the fort. At the age of seventeen, she was married to Alexander Smith, who lived in what is now Williamson County. With that event, the name of Leiper passes out, so far as represented by the line descending from Captain James Leiper.

"It is to be regretted that details are lacking for a fuller portraiture of this typical pioneer. We should like to know more of the intimate characteristics of the man. He was brave and daring. From that known fact, and the further fact that he was appreciated and esteemed by Robertson, we may reasonably infer that he was tender and true, and an upright man in heart and soul.

"Looking back upon the twilight of the dawn of our mighty Commonwealth, the figures of the pioneers loom large against the horizon. There is no real need for defter or finer strokes of portraiture; an inspiring silhouette suffices. They were nation-builders, and, among them, Captain James Leiper did his part, without fear and without reproach!"

Unveiled at Fort Nashborough May 1st, 1935.

On May 1, 1935, a ceremony in honor of Captain James Leeper took place in Nashville, at the reconstructed Fort Nashborough. A bronze placque was unveiled, the gift of Cumberland Chapter, Daughters of the American Revolution, Mrs. Armistead and Mrs. Walter Woolwine unveiling the memorial. J. Washington Moore, Esquire, City Attorney of Nashville, spoke on the occasion. He described the motives which brought about the settlement of this metropolis, then a wilderness. "Possibly the land-hunger that has always characterized civilized man, the love of home and all its connotes, the unquenchable desire for individual liberty and personal freedom, the spirit of adventure, the fondness for the chase, the love of nature, hope of fortune in a new country, yearning for illimitable opportunity, lust for conquest, all entered into and constituted that irrestible urge that compelled those hardy pioneers." Mr. Moore contrasted the dauntless spirit of Nashville's founders with the modern weakness and cowardice constituting such a present danger for our country. "In these times, when, as a people, we have become soft, when our courage and our initiative are suffering from a creep-

Copy of Captain James Leeper's original land grant.

ing paralysis, when our will to face with fortitude an unknown future is weakening, . . . it is well to have brought before us vividly the strength, the tough fibre, the high courage, indomitable will, unwavering fortitude, the unquestioning faith, and the boundless hope of these Signers of the Cumberland Compact."

The Cumberland Compact was drawn up and agreed upon when the settlers came to their new home in the wild mountains by the Cumberland River. Among the signatures are those of several whose families are described in this book: James Leeper, Hugh Leeper, George Leeper, John Drake, Jonathan Drake, Benjamin Drake, Isaac Drake, Frederick Stump.

The government of North Carolina had granted lands in the new country to the soldiers who went there to protect the settlements. Each Private was given four hundred acres for his first year's service, and a larger tract to each officer. Whether they constituted all of Captain James Leeper's land-holdings in Tennessee is not known, but six hundred and forty acres were allotted to his heirs by the State of North Carolina, which still claimed jurisdiction over the territory, June 26, 1793. The following document is recorded in the Land Grant Office, at Nashville, Tennessee, in Book G, on Page 184*.

"Number 388. Know ye, that we have granted unto the heirs of James Leeper six hundred forty acres of land in our county Davidson. Beginning at a honey locust and runs north crossing a branch one hundred eighty four poles, corners on a hackberry. John Henderson's south boundary four hundred and twenty poles. Thence, west crossing a branch at twelve poles and at one hundred and seventy two poles and cornered an elm and white oak at two hundred and eighty-one poles, four tenth, thence south crossing little Harper at sixty poles continued to James Crockett's line at three hundred and thirty piles, thence east to a black walnut, one hundred and seventy-five poles, thence south with said Crockett's line, ninety poles to a dogwood and elm, thence east to the beginning crossing little Harper at forty poles continued, to hold to the said heirs of James Leeper, their heirs and assigns forever.

---

*This is an incomplete and not strictly *verbatim* copy, as the original record, as may be seen by the engraved reproduction illustrating this book, is worn and torn with the ravages of time.

Dated June 26, 1793.

Warrant Number 142

William Collinsworth

Richard Dobbs Spaight

John Buchanan

George Leeper, C. C."

On this land doubtless would have been the home of Captain Leeper and his wife, and it would have become perhaps an ancestral homestead filled with their mementoes and belongings and with the memory of their long and happy life together, if their union on earth had been prolonged more than its few, short months. When they stood together to be married, in old Fort Nashborough, no shadow of the coming future—the wild fight, the chase, the din of howling dogs and screaming savages, followed by the silence of death,—darkened the scene. All nature seemed eager to add pleasure and beauty to their hearts' happiness. No artificial decorations were needed, for the grass made a green velvet carpet for the bride's tiny feet, and the wild-flowers added their bright colors as well as their fragrance. The birds in the leafy bowers overhead sang sweetly to their mates, and the great, gnarled forest-trees furnished shade. Even the river, rushing past below the fort, lapped its waves merrily against the mighty bluff, while, over all, was the blue, spreading canopy of Heaven.

This first wedding across the mountains must have been an occasion of supreme festivity to the little band of pioneers. While they knew the enjoyment of log-raising parties, when new homes were being built, quilting-bees, and other gaieties, this surpassed them all. All the settlers gathered around, attending the pair, soft strains of music by self-taught fiddlers floated through the fort and out into the forest. All was full of hope and happiness, for "love is sweet and they were young."

After the groom had kissed his bride and all had offered their congratulations, it is recorded that "there was pretty much of a feast spread in the fort." They had none of the delicacies of today, but enjoyed such substantial food as "fresh and dried meat, buffalo, tongue, bear-meat, venison, saddle and venison ham,—broiled, stewed, and jerked,—some roasting ears, or green corn, roasted, broiled, or made into succotash." According to tradition, they had also a wedding-cake, made by Mrs. McNairy.

Fort Nashborough

Even on such an occasion, the lurking Indian was not forgotten, and the men with their rifles were ever ready and alert; but we are glad to know that nothing happened to mar the pleasure of their happy day,—when James Leeper and Susan Drake became husband and wife. Soon enough, the peril then hidden became visible, tangible, a death-dealing reality.

Captain Leeper, living, as he did, in the midst of potential dangers, had known that sudden death was always to be faced. After receiving the wounds which were to prove mortal, in the Battle of the Bluffs, he took care to provide for his wife and for the unborn child which he and she then expected would soon enter their life. On April 16, 1781, he made his Will. An abridged copy of this document, now recorded in the Court House at Nashville, in Book 2, on Page 10, follows, its engraved reproduction appearing as an illustration of this book.

"I James Leper on Cumberland River in the State of North Carolina do This Sixteenth Day of Apl. in The Year of our Lord One Thousand Seven Hundred & Eighty One Make This My Last Will & Testament, Viz—

Item. That if My Welbeloved Wife Susannah be Now Pregnant with Child, That The Lands I have Entered In Hendersons Office May hereafter be Secured for it. If Otherwise That The S.d Lands be Secured The one Half for my Wife And The Other for My Father. And that all my Legal Debts be Satisfied. . . . I Also Appoint . . . James Robertson & Hugh Leper Executors of This My Last Will & Testament, ... In Witness Whereof I here Unto Set my hand Seal, ...

In presence of   James Leper (seal)
Andrew Ervin
Andrew Lucas
     his
Thomas ———— Spencer" (This last, an illegible signature, prob-
     Mark   ably as here written.)

Hugh Leeper, named as Executor, is said to have been Captain James Leeper's brother.

Copy of the original will of Captain James Leeper

There has been little learned authentically as to the Leeper family, either in America or abroad. The statement has been made that it was French, later settling in Ireland. It is true that the family did live in Ireland, and that County Down, in that country, is believed to have been the home of Allen Leeper, who was in Pennsylvania by 1744. He was born in 1720. It is also true that the origin of the name may very probably have been French. Perhaps the family came to England at the time of the Norman Conquest, or during the ensuing period when many Frenchmen settled in England. There does not appear reason, however, to think that it emigrated from France at a later time, or that Ireland was its first British home. Harrison, author of "Surnames of the United Kingdom," states its derivation from the word, "leaper," and perhaps derived from the Old English "hleapere," meaning a dancer, and, thence, a runner, a leaper. The name's spelling has been and is variant: Leeper, Lepper, Leaper, Leiper (used sometimes for the family of Captain James Leeper), Lepar, Leper, and other forms.

Sometimes, in England, the surname was prefixed by the French article, "Le,"—"The." William le Lepar is recorded in the reign of King Edward I; Alicia Lepar, in 1379; Geoffrey le Lepere, in Oxfordshire, 1273; John Leaper, who married Florence Dawson, in London, 1598-1599; Robert Leaper of Over Kellet, in Lancashire, 1611. Captain James Leeper, in his Will, signed his name and mentioned himself as "James Leper." It is probable, however, that most of the family in America, including his descendants of other surnames, have followed the spelling adopted in this book: "Leeper." That, doubtless, expresses its usual pronunciation.

In the 1700's there were members of the Leeper family in Pennsylvania and in Virginia, and, also, in North Carolina. Since Tennessee was then included in North Carolina, it is possibly more probable that Captain James Leeper's family had lived there. From the Captain's Will, described above, it is known that his father was then living, 1781, and, assumably, living in Tennessee; since no place of residence was mentioned for his father in the Will. Hugh Leeper is named in the Will as one of the Executors. Perhaps he was Captain James Leeper's father. Certainly, he was a kinsman. The statement has been made, but not authenticated, that Captain Leeper had a brother, Hugh, and other brothers, Andrew, George, and Thomas. In 1790, when the first census of the United States was taken, John and Moses Leeper were listed among the heads of households in what was then Morgan District, Lincoln County. This was in the western part of the State, near to what was to become Tennessee.

Drake

THE ORIGINAL HOME, in England, of the Drake family is said to have been at the present Musbury, in Devonshire. This had been the site of a military encampment in the Anglo-Roman period, and a family whose leader seems to have been Drago is believed to have settled there, after the Saxon Conquest of Britain in the Fifth Century. "Drago, the Saxon," is mentioned in Domesday Book, the record of English lands and owners made by William the Conqueror, soon after the Norman Conquest of 1066. This Drago is therein recorded as having held Honiton, in Devon, before the Normans came. Other lands in the Shire are listed in Domesday as held by Drago.

Susan Drake, wife of Captain James Leeper, is believed to have been descended from a brother of Sir Francis Drake, the famous Admiral and explorer of Queen Elizabeth's time. Therefore, the following pedigree is set forth, tracing the lineage in this ancient family akin to Sir Francis and his brothers, including Thomas Drake, ancestor, as stated, of Susan (Drake) Leeper.

John Drake, of Mount Drake (Musbury), Devonshire, married, in the first quarter of the Fifteenth Century, Christiana, daughter and heiress of John Billett of Ashe, in Devon. The Arms of Billett, or Billet, are blazoned: *Arms*—Argent, on a chief gules three cinquefoils of the field. *Crest*—A hand and arm couped at the elbow in armor proper, in the gauntlet a baton or. As will be shown, the Billet Crest was added to the Arms of Drake of Ashe, this seat coming to the Drake family through the said marriage of John Drake and Christiana Billet. The Coat-Armor of Drake of Ashe (called, by Burke, the well-known authority on British Armory, "a family of great antiquity"), is blazoned: *Arms*—Argent, a wivern, wings displayed and tail nowed, gules. *Crests*—(1) A dexter arm erect couped at the elbow proper, holding a battle-axe sable headed argent; (2) an eagle displayed gules. *Motto—Aquila non capit muscas.* This, in English, is: "The eagle does not catch flies."

John Drake, Second, son of John and Christiana (Billet) Drake, was of Otterton, Devonshire. His wife was Christiana, daughter and heiress of John Antage.

John Drake, Third, son of John and Christiana (Antage) Drake, married a daughter of John Cruwys, or Crews.

John Drake, Fourth, son of the preceding, lived at Otterton, and married Agnes, daughter of John Kailway. They had children: John, Johan (a daughter), Robert, Gilbert, and Thomas.

John Drake, Fifth, eldest son of John and Agnes (Kailway) Drake, was seated at Ashe and at Exmouth, in Devon. He married Margaret, daughter and heiress of John Cole, of Rill, in the Parish of Whytecombe Raleigh, Devon. John and Margaret (Cole) Drake had issue: John, John (a second son, of the same name, in accordance with a practice not unusual in olden times), Alice, and Gilbert.

John Drake, Sixth, eldest son of John and Margaret (Cole) Drake, was of Mount Drake, Ashe, and Exmouth. He was Sheriff of Devonshire in the time of Queen Mary, probably, and died October 4, 1558. He married Amy, daughter of Roger Greenville, of Stow, in Cornwall.

John and Amy (Greenville) Drake had two sons: Sir Barnard and Robert. From Sir Barnard Drake is said to have descended Thomas Drake, who came to Weymouth, Massachusetts, 1653. The line from Sir Barnard to Thomas is given as follows: John Drake, eighth son of Sir Barnard, and who married Dorothy Button; William Drake, second son of John and Dorothy, married Margaret Westover; Thomas Drake, baptized 1635, the colonist at Weymouth.

Another colonist of the family, John Drake, came to Boston, Massachusetts, 1630, was one of the Proprietors of Taunton, Massachusetts, and later settled at Windsor, Connecticut. He is thought to have been descended from the above-mentioned Robert Drake (brother of Sir Barnard), son of John Drake, Sixth, and the latter's wife, Amy Greenville. The lineage from Robert to John, the colonist, is given as follows: Robert, son of John and Amy, married Elizabeth Prideaux; William Drake, son of Robert and Elizabeth, married Philippa Denys; John Drake, son of William and Philippa, came to Massachusetts, 1630.

Returning to the specific ancestry, believed to have been that of Susan Drake, wife of Captain James Leeper, the pedigree begins with John Drake, of Crowndale, in Tavistock, Devonshire. His will was proved in 1566. The wife of John Drake was probably Margery Hawkins. They had children:

    i John Drake; died by 1567, when his Will was proved; probably left no issue.

- ii Edmond Drake; described presently.
- iii Robert Drake; married Anna Laxmore; had issue: John Drake, who became Page to Sir Francis Drake, his cousin; Dorothy Drake; Elizabeth Drake.
- iv John Drake; youngest son, and second son of the name; died in 1610.

Edmund Drake, second son of John and Margery (Hawkins) Drake, became a Chaplain in the British Navy, under Elizabeth. Later, he probably became Vicar of Upchurch, in County Kent. He died in 1596. The wife of Edmund Drake was a daughter of Richard Mylwaye.

The children of Edmund and ——— (Mylwaye) Drake were:
- i Sir Francis Drake, the great Admiral, who brought such glory to the reign of Queen Elizabeth; believed to have been born about 1545, but perhaps several years earlier; died in 1595; died, January 28, 1595, on board his ship, near the town, Nombre de Dios, in the West Indies; the first Englishman to sail around the world; knighted, for this and other exploits, by Queen Elizabeth; again set sail, renewing his victories against Spanish ships and ports; as Drake himself expressed it, "singed the King of Spain's beard," April 19, 1587, by sailing into Cadiz and destroying there ten thousand tons of shipping, planned as part of the great Spanish Armada for the conquest of England; when the Armada approached the English coast, captured one of its largest galleons; about this time was made Vice-Admiral; again took part in expeditions in the West Indies, where, as already said, he died; was Mayor of Plymouth, 1581; married twice, but left no children to grow up; one of the rich and exciting characters who made splendid "the spacious times of great Elizabeth," and a glory of England forever.
- ii John Drake.
- iii Edmund Drake, Junior.
- iv Joseph Drake.
- v Thomas Drake; described below.

Thomas Drake, just mentioned, of Buckland Abbey, was the youngest son of Reverend Edmund Drake, and brother of Sir

Francis Drake, the Admiral. He was born in 1556, and died April 4, 1606. In 1587, he married Elizabeth Gregory, who died in March, 1631-1632.

It should be said that there is much confusion concerning the lists of children of Thomas and following ancestors in this lineage, so far as it has been set forth in an English work on the subject, "The Family and Heirs of Sir Francis Drake," by Lady Eliott-Drake. A careful study of this and other material on the family, including the official Heralds' Visitations, indicates, however, a clear pedigree, from Thomas Drake down. Therefore, from hence to the American history of the family, only the record of direct ancestors will be given.

Sir Francis Drake, eldest son of Thomas and Elizabeth (Gregory) Drake, was baptized September 16, 1588. He was created a Baronet. He died on March 11, 1637. Sir Francis married twice. His first wife was Jane, daughter of Sir Amias Bamfield. She died in February, 1613. Although there seems no doubt that the family line was carried down through his second marriage, nevertheless, as will be shown, the surname, Bamfield, was handed down as a Baptismal name. Sir Francis' second marriage was to Joan, daughter of Sir William Strode. Only one child appears to have been born of his first marriage, Dorothy, who died in infancy.

Joseph Drake, youngest son of Sir Francis and Joan (Strode) Drake, was seated at Upperton, in Buckland, Devonshire. He died in October, 1708. In 1668, he married Margaret, daughter of Ludovic Crymes. His second wife was baptized Grace, but her maiden-surname is unknown.

Reverend Bamfield Drake was the only son, leaving issue, of Joseph and Margaret (Crymes) Drake. He was Rector of the Parish of Farway, in Devon. He married, but his wife's name is unknown. As it is strongly indicated that Susan Drake, wife of Captain James Leeper, descended from Reverend Bamfield Drake, full record will be set down here of known facts concerning his children. They were as follows:

    i John Drake; Mayor of Plymouth; died in 1753; married Ann Spicer; had children:

        1 John Drake; a Lieutenant in the 33rd Regiment; is said to have died without issue.

        2 Catherine Drake; married Captain Rogers of the Royal Navy.

ii　Joseph Drake; died without issue, it is stated.
　　iii　Francis Drake; described below.
　　iv　Bamfield Drake, Junior; described below.

Lady Eliott-Drake, above-mentioned historian of the family in England, connected with Sir Francis Drake, the great Admiral, writes, concerning the branch (just traced herein), from Joseph and Margaret (Crymes) Drake, of which branch, as shown above, only Francis and Bamfield (sons of Reverend Bamfield Drake), could have carried down the lineage to later generations bearing the surname, Drake: "Little is known about this branch of the family; their descendants, it is said, went to America."

One Drake family, early in North Carolina, later in Kentucky, and, afterwards, in other Southern States, descended from the said Reverend Bamfield Drake, although, in the course of time, this name became, in their tradition, "Bamfylde." Possibly this was the original form. A descendant of this branch, writing in 1914, said: "We have Bible records and proofs of dates of birth, marriage, etc., of this line." Their line, they trace from the above-described Thomas Drake, youngest brother of Sir Francis Drake, the Admiral, down to Francis, son of Reverend Bamfield Drake, as noted above. This Francis, they state, married Mary Buckingham, and had a son, James Drake. James Drake had a son, Albrittain Drake, born in Devonshire, but who came to North Carolina, as, also, seems to have come his father, James. Study of the lineage from this James Drake will appear subsequently herein.

Francis Drake, son of Reverend Bamfield Drake, may, therefore, be considered as ancestor of one American Drake lineage. It appears extremely probable that, either from him, or from his brother, Bamfield Drake, Junior, descended Susan Drake, wife of Captain James Leeper.

According to an old family-chart, the grandfather of Susan (Drake) Leeper was John Drake, who married, in Devonshire, Margaret Weldon. So far as dates are known, or can be surmised, it appears that he might have been a brother of the aforesaid James, son of Francis and Mary (Buckingham) Drake; or it may be that John who married Margaret Weldon was descended from this Francis Drake's brother, Bamfield Drake, Junior, mentioned above herein.

The statement of Lady Eliott-Drake, cited above, the fact that one Drake lineage in America has record of its descent from Thomas, brother of Sir Francis Drake, the Admiral, down to Albrittain Drake, of North Carolina, and the fact that descendants of Susan (Drake) Leeper state that they descend from a brother of Sir Francis Drake, the Admiral, all appear to indicate, in the strongest way, that the ancestral line of Susan Drake, wife of Captain James Leeper, was as follows:

JOHN DRAKE, of Crowndale, in Tavistock, Devonshire, England, and his wife, probably Margery Hawkins.

REVEREND EDMUND DRAKE, Vicar of Upchurch, in Kent, who died in 1596, and his wife, ——— Mylwaye.

THOMAS DRAKE, youngest brother of the great Admiral, Sir Francis Drake, born 1556, died 1606, and his wife, married in 1587, Elizabeth Gregory, this ancestor seated at Buckland Abbey, Devonshire.

SIR FRANCIS DRAKE, first Baronet, died 1637, and his second wife, Joan, daughter of Sir William Strode.

JOSEPH DRAKE, youngest son of the first Baronet, of Upperton, in Buckland, Devon, died 1708, and his first wife, married in 1668, Margaret, daughter of Ludovic Crymes.

REVEREND BAMFIELD DRAKE, Rector of Farway Parish, Devonshire, and his wife, whose name is unknown.

> FRANCIS DRAKE, son of Reverend Bamfield Drake, and his wife, Mary Buckingham, *or* BAMFIELD DRAKE, JUNIOR, son of Reverend Bamfield Drake.

It seems perhaps more probable that the line came down, from this point, to Susan Drake, through the said Francis, son of Reverend Bamfield Drake,—rather than from the latter's other son, Bamfield Drake, Junior. If this surmise is correct, then the abovementioned John Drake, grandfather of Susan (Drake) Leeper, would have been brother to James Drake, whose son, Albrittain Drake, born in Devonshire, came to North Carolina, as has already been mentioned.

Continuing the direct pedigree, from John Drake to Crowndale, Tavistock, Devon (grandfather of Sir Francis, the Admiral), to Susan Drake:

> JOHN DRAKE, son either of Francis and Mary (Buckingham) Drake, or of Francis' brother, Bamfield Drake, Junior (whose wife's name is unknown), married Margaret Weldon.

BENJAMIN DRAKE, of North Carolina and Tennessee, and his wife, perhaps Susan ———.

SUSAN DRAKE, whose marriage to Captain James Leeper, 1780, was the first celebrated in old Fort Nashborough, the present Nashville, Tennessee.

Susan (Drake) Leeper, thus, would have been of the Tenth Generation, beginning with John Drake of Crowndale, aforesaid.

John Drake and his wife, Margaret Weldon, grandparents of Susan Drake, had the following children:

 i Jonathan Drake; described subsequently.
 ii Enoch Drake.
 iii John Drake; described subsequently.
 iv Samuel Drake; described subsequently.
 v Mary Drake; married James Null.
 vi Margaret Drake; described subsequently.
 vii Benjamin Drake; described subsequently.

It is believed that records of Benjamin, John, and Jonathan Drake, in North Carolina, in the Seventeen Hundreds, refer to three sons of these names, listed as above in the family of John and Margaret (Weldon) Drake.

Benjamin Drake had land on the Yadkin River, North Carolina, 1755. John Drake's name also appears in connection with land ownership in the same locality. Jonathan Drake was nominee for the rank of Major, as an officer of the Militia, as Commissioner of Building, and Commissioner of Salt.*

---

*North Carolina Colonial Records: Volume 5, Page 494; Volume 20, Pages 566 and 125; Volume 24, Pages 617 and 915.

Jonathan Drake

IN THE 1780's, there were two men, named Jonathan Drake, in Tennessee. One came from North Carolina, and one from Virginia, but it is indicated that they were related, as their descendants considered each other kinfolks. It is thought possible that Jonathan, from North Carolina, was identical with Jonathan, above-mentioned son of John and Margaret (Weldon) Drake.

The North Carolina Jonathan, as mentioned above, was Building Commissioner (at Nashville, from Nashborough, 1784), and Salt Commissioner. As a soldier of the Revolution, he was given a tract of six hundred and forty acres, on the north side of the Cumberland River, in Davidson County. This land is said to remain in the possession of his descendants. It is about ten miles from Nashville. As said above, he was nominee for Major, and he received that rank. This Jonathan Drake married, and had a daughter, Sarah Drake. She married Joseph Hardin, Junior, about 1795. The latter was son of Major Joseph Hardin (born, in Virginia, April 18, 1734, and died in Hardin Valley, Tennessee, July 4, 1801), a soldier of the Revolution, who received for his service three thousand acres in the present Hardin County, Tennessee, then part of North Carolina, in whose forces he had fought.

Before continuing the record of descendants of this Jonathan Drake, through his daughter, Sarah (Drake) Hardin, notice will be given, as follows, concerning the other Jonathan Drake, mentioned above as an early settler in Tennessee, and who came there from Virginia. He made his home in Montgomery County, Tennessee, and there died, about 1804. In Davidson County records (Deed Book F, Page 185), is a conveyance, dated August 16, 1804, of twenty-four acres of land on White's Creek, to Isaac Drake. The grantors were Robert Drake, Prudence Drake, A. Stuart, and Matthew Ryburn, all the heirs of Jonathan Drake, deceased, of Montgomery County. These heirs, May 22, 1805, deeded to Christopher Strong two hundred acres on White's Creek (Book F, Page 250), this land having been conveyed to them, as Jonathan Drake's heirs, by William White, of North Carolina, May 18, 1805 (Book G, Page 75).

Returning to the lineage descending from Jonathan Drake, Revolutionary soldier of North Carolina, who settled near Nashville, Tennessee, and who appears to have been identical with Jonathan, son of John and Margaret (Weldon) Drake:

His daughter, Sarah Drake, mentioned above, was born in 1777, and her marriage to Joseph Hardin, Junior, took place about 1795. They had the following children:

    i   Benjamin Hardin; killed, while a boy, by the Indians.

    ii   Jonathan Hardin; removed to Arkansas in 1820.

    iii Prudence Hardin; married Ira Nash; removed, about 1827, either to Texas, then a part of Mexico, or to some other part of Mexico, where her husband was killed.

    iv Joab Hardin; married Amy Dillahunty, 1832; had one child.

          Sarah Ann Hardin; married Leonard Lane Leech, October 31, 1852; had issue:

          1 Ernest Leech; married Florence Collier.

          2 Hardin Leech; married Loulie Leech.

          3 Early Leech; married Lizzie Morris.

          4 Blake Leech; married Beulah McLean.

          5 Varrie Leech; married John L. Neely,* Assistant Attorney-General of Tennessee; had children: John Neely, who married Louise Cook; Leonard Neely, who married Rebekah Lyle Ewing; Elizabeth Neely, who married Wade Hampton Tisdale.

---

*"Nestledown," the ancestral home of the Neely family, is near Franklin, Tennessee. It has been in the family possession for five generations.

John Drake

JOHN DRAKE, indicated as identical with John, son of John and Margaret (Weldon) Drake, received, as noted above, land on the Yadkin River, in North Carolina. On April 17, 1786, a grant was made to him, by the State of North Carolina, of a tract of six hundred and forty acres in what was then Davidson County, North Carolina, now in Tennessee. This land lay "on the north side of Cumberland River and upon the White's Creek." The grant was signed by Richard Caswell, James Malherin, Benjamin Drake, and Frederick Stump, C. C. This Benjamin Drake was doubtless Benjamin, brother of John, while both were sons of John and Margaret (Weldon) Drake, as there seems no question.

Samuel Drake

JOHN DRAKE and his wife, Margaret Weldon, as noted, and as recorded in the Drake Family Chart, which has been mentioned herein, had a son, Samuel Drake. He was the uncle of Susan Drake, wife of Captain James Leeper. Descendants of the last-mentioned couple and descendants of a certain Samuel Drake (to be described presently), call each other "cousins." Therefore, it may be that the following Samuel Drake was identical with Samuel, uncle of Susan (Drake) Leeper.

Samuel Drake was born in 1719. He married, first, Margaret Pottle, and, second, Mary Cox, in 1743. As he was then only twenty-four years old, it is probable that all, or nearly all, his children were born of his second marriage. They were as follows:

i Joseph Drake; perhaps identical with Joseph Drake, who came, first, to Tennessee, in 1769, coming then, it is said, from western Virginia, returning several times, and marrying in Tennessee, 1773, Margaret Buchannon; this last Joseph Drake killed in 1778, leaving a son, John, of Bedford County, Tennessee, 1809.

ii Ephraim Drake; married Ann Richardson; had a son, Joseph Drake; perhaps identical with the Ephraim Drake, related to above-mentioned Joseph Drake (thought identical with Joseph, son of Samuel Drake), apparently as younger brother, but who married Anna Buchannon (sister of said Joseph's wife), and was living in Bedford County, Tennessee, 1809.

iii Samuel Drake; married Pauline Cox; had daughter, Mary Drake, who married —— Jackson, and had a son, Isaac Jackson.

iv Nathaniel Drake; married Mary Jackson; had a son, Isaac Drake, and a daughter, Mary Drake. (See, below, "Isaac Drake.")

v Mary Drake; married, 1771-1772, James Crockett, born 1750, in Wythe County (then Augusta County), Virginia, who died in 1826, and was son of Samuel and Esther (Thompson) Crockett; he doubtless identical with James Crockett, who, April 17, 1786, was granted by North Carolina six hundred and forty acres "on South fork of little Harpeth," in Tennessee (then in Davidson County, North Carolina); had children:

    1 Sallie Crockett; born July 6, 1773; died in 1854; married Thomas Harbert, June 3, 1792.

    2 John D. Crockett; born in 1775; died in 1856; did not marry.

    3 Samuel Crockett; married Nancy Craig.

    4 Mary Drake Crockett; born May 23, 1778; died in November, 1826; married, April 24, 1799, James McGavock, Junior, born June 10, 1764, the son of James McGavock, Senior, and died May 12, 1838.

    5 Esther Crockett; born in January, 1780; died July 9, 1870; married Francis Jackson Carter.

    6 James Crockett, Junior; born in 1782; died in 1862; married Nancy Friel.

    7 Ephraim Crockett; born in 1784; did not marry.

    8 Stephen Crockett; born in 1787; did not marry.

    9 Abraham Crockett; born in 1791; died in 1827.

    10 Nathaniel Crockett; born in 1792; died in 1870; married Mary Graham.

    11 Elizabeth Crockett; born September 7, 1795; died January 31, 1862; married Lysander McGavock, December 5, 1832; he was born October 22, 1800, the son of David McGavock.

vi Rebecca Drake; married William Newell; had daughters: Betsy, who married ——— Duncannon ("Thuncannon"); Thirza ("Thursa"), who married George ———; Lenah, who married Andrew Sanders.

vii William Drake; mentioned in the Will of Samuel Drake, his father, cited below.

viii Elizabeth Drake; mentioned in the Will of Samuel Drake as Elizabeth Daugherty (probably her married name), apparently as the testator's daughter, and also seemingly identical with "Effie," mentioned in Samuel Drake's Will.

  ix Rachel Drake; married ——— Shepherd; mentioned in Samuel Drake's Will as "my daughter Rachel Shepherd."

  x Margaret Drake; called Margaret Livingston, in Samuel Drake's Will, and apparently his daughter.

  xi Sarah Drake; called by her first name only in the Will of Samuel Drake, and apparently his daughter.

The Will of Samuel Drake is recorded in the Court House at Nashville. An abstract of this document follows:

"In the first place I will and bequeath unto my son Ephram Drake one negro boy named Ned, and in the second place to Elizabeth Daugherty the sum of one dollar. To Mary Crockett the sum of one dollar. To my daughter Rebecca Newell one dollar. To my daughter Rachel Shepherd one dollar. To Margaret Livingston one negro girl Luce she has in her possession.

"In the third place I give and bequeath unto my two sons Nathaniel and William Drake my whole lands entaile to be equally and impartially divided among them.

"It is my desire and intention that after the death of my wife her part of the slaves should be divided equally among Nathanial, William, Sarah, and Effie. My three sons, Ephram, Nathaniel, and William Drake to be executors of this my last will and testament. Lastly I desire that my estate may not be appraised as witness my hand and seal this 6th day of December A.D. 1795.

"Samuel Drake."

It seems probable that Samuel Drake had already made some division of his property among all, or part, of his children, since only a few of them are mentioned in this Will, and, of these few, some received thereby only the token of a dollar. Doubtless, all had received actually some share in their father's estate before his Will was made.

Margaret Drake

AMONG THE CHILDREN, listed above herein, of John and Margaret (Weldon) Drake, was Margaret, also called, Margaret Weldon Drake, who married General John B. South. He entered and owned several tracts of land in Kentucky, receiving these grants about 1784. He died in 1819.

The children of General John B. and Margaret (Drake) South were:

    i Colonel John South; a soldier of the Revolutionary War; married Betsy, daughter of William Hay, Mayor of Richmond, Virginia; resided near Richmond; had children:

        1 John South, Junior.
        2 Thomas South.
        3 Parthenia South.
        4 Elizabeth South.
        5 Judith South.
        6 Elgion (Elgin?) South.
        7 Theodosia South.
        8 Sallie South.
        9 Margaret South.

    ii Colonel Samuel South; a Revolutionary soldier; married, and had (perhaps with other children), a son: William King South, who married Mary Ann Glover, and had twelve children, among them a son, ——— South (father of Doctor John F. South, of McDaniels, Kentucky), and a daughter, Sally South, who married ——— Smallwood, and had children.

Benjamin Drake

BENJAMIN DRAKE, son of John and Margaret (Weldon) Drake, was the father of Susan Drake, who married Captain James Leeper. He was born in 1730, whether in America or England being unknown. He is the first recorded ancestor of the lineage who could have been born in America, his parents' marriage having taken place in Devonshire, according to the old family-chart which has been mentioned before.

As already stated, it is believed that he held land, in 1755, on the Yadkin River, in North Carolina. He served as Guard to the State Commissioners of North Carolina who laid out the tracts allotted to the Revolutionary officers and soldiers serving in the Continental Line of the State. As compensation for this, which, in those frontier-days of peril from the Indians and hardships of the wilderness, must have been active and dangerous service, Benjamin Drake received a grant of three hundred and twenty acres in Tennessee. The survey of this land was dated, it appears, August 15, 1785.

On April 17, 1786, the State of North Carolina granted him a larger tract, containing six hundred and forty acres of land, "lying and being in White's Creek." (Deed Book G, Page 88, Warrant Number 64.)

The Baptismal name and the maiden surname of Benjamin Drake's wife are both unknown. Since their only known daughter was named Susan, it may be that this was also the mother's name. When she married Benjamin Drake, she was a widow, her first husband having been ——— Smith.

The children of Benjamin Drake and his wife were:

    i Benjamin Drake, Junior; described subsequently.

    ii Jonathan Drake. (See, herein, the Criddle family history.)

    iii John Drake; born in 1761; married Elizabeth Rounceville.

    iv Susan Drake; described subsequently.

Benjamin Drake, Junior, son of Benjamin Drake, was born in 1758. He made his Will on April 6, 1831, and in this document (recorded in Davidson County Court House, Nashville, Tennessee,*

---
*Book 9, Page 513.

under proceedings of the Court sessions in July, 1831, which fixes his death as between April 6 and July, 1831), he is called Benjamin I. Drake. A copy of this Will follows.

"In the Name of God Amen.

I, Benjamin I. Drake of Davidson County and State of Tennessee, being in a low state of health in body, but of sound mind and memory and calling to mind the mortality of my body and knowing it is appointed unto all men once to die do therefore make this my last will and testament. In the following manner, that is to say, first of all, I recommend my soul to God and my body to be decently buried at the direction of my Executors and as touching such worldly estate as it has pleased God to bless me with in this world, I dispose of in the following manner to wit: My will is that my Executors shall first, pay all my just debts if any such there be. I give and bequeath to my grandson Benjamin Franklin Drake all my land which I own, which lies south of the tract of land I have given and conveyed unto my son, William I. Drake, and joining the lines of Benjamin and Richard Hyde, John Drake and Thomas Smith, also all the land which I own that lies east of the tract I have conveyed to my son William as above stated, and the lands belonging to the heirs of Christopher Stump and Alexander Lester, containing fifty acres more or less. The last described pieces of land he shall have when of age. I give and bequeath to my daughter Sarah Drake who married James Powell, but now divorced, three negroes by name Patience, Primee and Mary. I give and bequeath to my grandson James Ford Drake, one negro man named Douglass. I give and bequeath to my granddaughter, Judith Adeline Marshall, one negro girl between fourteen and fifteen years of age to be purchased by my Executor or Executors out of my estate. I give and bequeath to the children of my son William I. Drake, which he now has or may have, except his son Benjamin Franklin Drake, whom I have already provided for, a negro woman named Zilicy, and her two children Squire and Bill, and all her increase to be equally divided among them or at the discretion of their father. I give and bequeath to my son William I. Drake, one negro man by the name of Lewis. It is my will that the negroes bequeathed to my daughter Sarah Drake, she shall have and all their increase also, at my death and the death of my wife Susannah Drake. I give and bequeath to my son William I. Drake all the residue of my estate of every description whatsoever which has not been mentioned in my will. I do appoint my son William I. Drake my sole Executor to this my last will and

Testament, hereby revoking all other wills or testaments by ratifying this as my last. In testimony whereof I have hereunto set my hand and seal this 6th day of April 1831."

The wife of the testator was Susanna Ramsey. Their children were as follows:

    i   Ephraim Drake; described subsequently.
   ii   Benjamin Drake.
  iii   Thirza Drake.
   iv   Sarah Drake; described subsequently.
    v   William I. Drake; described subsequently.
   vi   Lucretia Drake.

Ephraim Drake, son of Benjamin Drake, Junior, and the latter's wife, Susanna (Ramsey) Drake, predeceased his father, making his own Will on December 2, 1816, and dying between then and the January Court, 1817, when it was proved. He appointed "my loving father Benjamin Drake and my loving brother William I. Drake my Executors to this my last will and testament." He provided that clothing, which had belonged to his wife (evidently not then living), should be divided among his three daughters, "whenever they become of age or marry," and his son, James Ford Drake, also then a minor, was to have his own clothing. All his lands and personal property were to be divided among his four children. The daughters were not named in their father's will.

Sarah Drake, daughter of Benjamin Drake, Junior, and Susanna (Ramsey) Drake, married James (possibly, Joseph) Powell. They had children:

    i   Lucretia Powell; married Thomas Allison; had daughter, Rhoda Ann Allison.
   ii   Betsy Powell; married Louis Williams; had son, Benjamin Williams.
  iii   Edmund Powell; married Julia David; had sons, James Powell, and Edmund Powell, Junior.

William I. Drake, son of Benjamin, Junior, and Susanna (Ramsey) Drake, married Mary Bosley, and had children:

    i   Benjamin Franklin Drake; married Juliana Green; had issue:
        1   Susan Drake; married T. Young; had Ethel and Ida.

       2 Albert Drake; married Emma Biles; had daughter, Margaret Drake.
       3 Tennessee Drake; married H. Nance.
       4 Robert Drake; married Susie Truett; had son, Benjamin Drake.
       5 Clinton Drake.
       6 Mittie Drake; married S. Daly.
       7 Elvis Drake; married Catherine Williams; had Juliana, Edward, and Blanche Drake.
       8 Boyd Drake; married Effie Hyde; had daughter, Elizabeth J. Drake, who married C. A. Watkins and had issue, Martha Hyde Watkins and Charles Franklin Watkins.

ii Susan Drake; married T. Walton; had children: William J. Walton, who died young; Lizzie Walton; Ella Walton, who married J. King; Ernest T. Walton, who married Maggie ———; and Eugenia Walton.

iii John B. Drake; married Chloe Reed; had issue: William H. Drake, who married Laura Brodie; Clara Drake, who married W. Wilkerson; Sara Drake, who married B. Bratton; Mary Drake, who married E. Allen; Maud M. Drake; Joseph H. Drake; and John Drake.

iv James R. Drake; married Nancy Wilkerson, September 12, 1849; had Fannie, Laura, William, and Robert Drake.

v Elizabeth Drake; married Allen Ledbetter; had issue: Maud Ledbetter, who married H. Hunt; Joseph Ledbetter, who married ——— Edwards.

vi Harriet Drake; December 4, 1854, became second wife of her brother-in-law, Allen Ledbetter; had daughters, Susan D. and Mary E. Ledbetter.

Susan Drake

SUSAN DRAKE (whose brothers and their descendants have now been described herein), was the only-known daughter of Benjamin Drake, who was son of John and Margaret (Weldon) Drake. She was born in 1763, undoubtedly in North Carolina. Brought by her father to the future State of Tennessee, she was the first bride to be married in old Fort Nashborough, now Nashville, Tennessee. This event, which took place in the summer of 1780, has already been described herein. As also detailed above, this marriage was soon brought to a sorrowful end by the death of Susan Drake's brave husband, Captain James Leeper, mortally wounded at the Battle of the Bluff, in April, 1781.

About three years after Captain Leeper's death, Susan, his wife, was killed by the accidental discharge of a gun, which fell from its rack over a door. Her body was laid to rest beside that of her husband.

One child was born of the marriage of Captain James and Susan (Drake) Leeper. This was Sarah Jane Leeper, born in the summer of 1781, some three months after her father had been killed by the Indians. She lived to advanced age, dying in 1866. Her great-granddaughter, Elizabeth (Clack) Armistead, remembers her as a beautiful old lady who came to visit in the old Hadley home. Mrs Armistead's mother was Emeline Hadley and the Hadley mansion was built on land inherited by Captain Leeper's heirs. Part of this land is now owned by Mrs. Armistead.

After her mother's death, little Sarah Jane Leeper was brought up by an uncle, probably Benjamin Drake, Junior, account of whom appears above herein. When she was seventeen years old, she married Alexander Smith. Record of her descendants will be given subsequently, under the chronicle of the Smith family.

Isaac Drake

ISAAC DRAKE is believed to have been a son of Nathaniel Drake, who was son of Samuel Drake, the last being son of John and Margaret (Weldon) Drake, who were grandparents of Susan Drake, wife of Captain James Leeper. All of these have been described above herein. It has seemed advisable, for the sake of clarity, to narrate what is known of Isaac Drake and his descendants in this present, separate division of this book, and also herein to supplement the foregoing account of Nathaniel Drake, believed, as said, to have been father of Isaac Drake of present consideration.

As already set forth, Samuel Drake (believed grandfather of Isaac), was born in 1719, was married, first, to Margaret Pottle, and, second, in 1743, when he was still only twenty-four years old, to Mary Cox. If his son, Nathaniel, was father of Isaac, born in 1756, it is indicated that Nathaniel must have been born of his father's very early marriage to Margaret Pottle, and that Nathaniel also married at an early age. This reasoning is based on the fact that Isaac Drake was born in 1756, making the births of three generations,—Samuel (born in 1719), Nathaniel, and Isaac (born in 1756),—take place within the short period of only thirty-seven years. In those pioneer days, however, very early marriages were common.

As already mentioned also, Nathaniel Drake (son of Samuel), married Mary Jackson, and they had, besides Isaac, a daughter, Mary Drake. It is probable that this Nathaniel was identical with Nathaniel Drake who, August 29, 1797, married Peggy Curd. The fact that, by his marriage to Mary Jackson, he had only two children, indicates that she had died early in their married life. By his second marriage, to Peggy Curd, Nathaniel Drake had the following children:

    i   Polly Drake; born June 21, 1798; married Thomas Jackson, February 27, 1823.

    ii   Patsy Drake; born October 25, 1802.

    iii   Edmund Drake; born February 14, 1804.

    iv   Joseph Drake; born August 17, 1806; married Patsy Chambers, June 17, 1828; had children:

        1   Mary S. Drake; born March 11, 1831.

        2   George W. Drake; born March 14, 1836.

        3   Joseph Drake; born in September, 1841.

v Samuel Drake; born November 13, 1808.
vi Sallie Drake; born February 5, 1811; married Joseph Haydon, in November, 1822.

If Nathaniel Drake, father of these children, was identical with Nathaniel Drake, believed father of Isaac Drake, they would have been half-brothers and half-sisters of Isaac, although about half a century younger than he.

Isaac Drake was born in 1756, and died May 13, 1815. On July 10, 1788, he had received, from the State of North Carolina, a grant of six hundred and forty acres of land in the present State of Tennessee. This estate lay in Davidson County, "on the waters of Pages creek, a branch of Big Harpeth River." The grant is recorded in Nashville, under Warrant Number 128, in Book G, Page 118.

Eight days before his death, Isaac Drake made his Will, May 5, 1815, and it was recorded on August 17, 1815, at Nashville. His wife had evidently pre-deceased him, as she was not mentioned in the Will, which named his eight children, in the order given below. The first, he called "my daughter Polly Curtis." The Will shows that his son, Logan, was not then twenty-one years of age.

Isaac Drake's wife was Jane Todd, of Kentucky. Their children follow:

i Polly Drake; married ——— Curtis.
ii Elizabeth Drake; married Laban Abernathy, February 22, 1819.
iii Logan Drake; a minor in 1815.
iv Joseph Drake; described subsequently.
v Amelia Drake; Will made June 2, 1820, proved September 4, 1820.
vi Rachel Drake; described subsequently.
vii Jane Drake; perhaps married Charles Abernathy.
viii Sallie Drake.

Joseph* Drake, son of Isaac and Jane (Todd) Drake, though named, in his father's Will, after Logan Drake, his brother, was, nevertheless, evidently the elder son. As said, Isaac's Will showed that Logan, then, was under age, while Joseph Drake was named, by his father, in this Will, "to administer on my estate." With

---
*Sometimes called Jesse.

him, in the work of settling the estate, Isaac Drake chose "Limus Tate."

Joseph was then actually thirty-one years of age. He was born on April 17, 1784, near Nashville, Tennessee. He died May 13, 1866. His wife was Rhoda Eddington, and they were married September 6, 1817. She was born December 27, 1800, and died March 4, 1884.

The children of Joseph and Rhoda (Eddington) Drake were:
  i Isaac W. Drake; described subsequently.
  ii Thomas E. Drake; born December 9, 1819; died August 12, 1870.
  iii Joseph B. Drake; born February 11, 1821; died March 7, 1849.
  iv Andrew Drake; born March 19, 1826; died July 16, 1827.
  v Helen Drake; born September 12, 1828; died February 4, 1892.
  vi William Drake; born in 1831; died February 18, 1884.
  vii Edwin Drake; born March 19, 1836; died June 5, 1863.

Isaac W. Drake, eldest of the foregoing children of Joseph and Rhoda (Eddington) Drake, was born June 2, 1818. He died August 27, 1899.

On June 11, 1836, he married Rhoda L. Neely, and their home was at Waverly, Tennessee, which remained his home after his second marriage also. This took place June 11, 1876, his second wife being Martha Ann Womble.

The children of Isaac W. Drake and Rhoda L. (Neely) Drake were:
  i Sarah Drake; born April 12, 1841; died March 4, 1908; married William Gatlin, in March, 1857, and had children:
    1 Jesse Gatlin; born September 7, 1858; married Mattie Cannida, February 14, 1880; had four children.
    2 Mary Gatlin; born November 12, 1860.
    3 John Gatlin; born October 12, 1862; married, and had several children; died October 29, 1891.
    4 Hick Gatlin; born April 9, 1866; married, and had a daughter, Elsie Gatlin.

- 5 Rhoda Gatlin; born April 10, 1867; married Henry Turner, January 27, 1904; had one child.
- 6 William W. Gatlin; born May 1, 1868; married Edna Henly, in September, 1885.
- 7 Charles Gatlin; born September 9, 1871; married Nellie Edwards, June 6, 1892.
- 8 Thomas W. Gatlin; born February 12, 1874; died March 20, 1896.
- 9 James A. Gatlin; born January 29, 1876; married Ellen Jones, August 18, 1898.
- 10 Harris Gatlin; born November 4, 1877; married Lucy Hoolilian, October 26, 1899.
- 11 Nannie Gatlin; born February 12, 1880; married Harris Harber, June 10, 1904.
- 12 Forest Gatlin; born August 16, 1881; married Lizzie Gavin, November 7, 1903.

ii Margaret Drake; born August 29, 1842; died in 1878; married James Holenbeck; had children, James and Sarah Holenbeck.

The children of Isaac W. Drake, by his second marriage, to Martha Ann Womble, were:

iii Calphurina Drake; known as "Callie"; born October 22, 1877; married Herman D. Skeggs, February 10, 1897, at Nashville, Tennessee; has children:
- 1 Pauline H. Skeggs; born June 13, 1898; died May 20, 1899.
- 2 Herman D. Skeggs, Junior; born May 3, 1901; died August 24, 1914.
- 3 Joseph Drake Skeggs; married Janie Pinson.

iv Joseph E. Drake; born December 23, 1879.

Descendants of Rachel (Drake) Abernathy

RACHEL DRAKE has been listed above as daughter of Isaac and Jane (Todd) Drake. She was born about 1785, and died in 1850. On January 18, 1816, in Davidson County, Tennessee, she married Freeman Abernathy.

Children of Freeman and Rachel (Drake) Abernathy:
- i Harmon Abernathy; children unknown.
- ii Martha Abernathy; described subsequently.
- iii Mastin C. Abernathy; described subsequently.
- iv Emily J. Abernathy; described subsequently.
- v Mary Abernathy; described subsequently.
- vi Jesse Logan Abernathy; described subsequently.
- vii Laban Abernathy; left no children.

Martha Abernathy, daughter of Freeman and Rachel (Drake) Abernathy, was born June 26, 1817, and did June 14, 1859. She married, as his second wife, in Davidson County, Tennessee, January 5, 1837, Charles Joel Herrin. He was born June 7, 1804, and died in 1889.

The children of Charles Joel and Martha (Abernathy) Herrin were as follows:
- i Emma Herrin; married Marshall McLean; had issue:
    1. Marcus McLean; of Lampasas, Texas.
    2. Cora McLean.
    3. Ella McLean.
    4. Emma McLean.
- ii Amanda Fitzallen Herrin; described subsequently.
- iii James Herrin; married Mary Welch, at West Point, Tennessee; had issue:
    1. Horace Herrin; married Bessie Blair, at West Point, Tennessee; had a son, Horace Herrin, Junior.
    2. Emma Herrin; married, first, John Pride; second, —— Lynch; had children, Lucile and James Pride.
    3. May Herrin; married William Porter; resides at Russellville, Alabama; children, Mary Ellen Por-

ter, William Porter, Junior, James Porter, and Dorothy Porter, all of whom are married.

    4 Frank Herrin; deceased; was married.

    5 Maude Herrin; married Gorman Nance; has daughter, Jane Nance.

    6 Linnie Herrin; married William Gilmore; resides at Louisville, Kentucky.

iv Frank Herrin; married Mary Lucind; has children:

    1 Maude Herrin; married John Hughes, of Fort Worth, Texas; has children, Horace and John Hughes.

    2 Linnie Herrin; of Graham, Texas.

v Charles F. Herrin; practised medicine at West Point, Tennessee; died, unmarried.

vi Ella Herrin; married N. M. Hollis, West Point, Tennessee; both deceased; had children:

    1 Minnie Lawrence Hollis; deceased; married John Embry, of Florence, Alabama; had children, John Marcus Embry and Julia Embry, who married Ira Parks, of Union City, Tennessee, and has two daughters.

    2 Jeannette Hollis; married Roy Welch, West Point, Tennessee; had children, Catherine and William Welch.

    3 Buford Hollis; deceased; married Ruth Dixon; two children.

    4 Blanche Hollis; married ———— ————.

Amanda Fitzallen Herrin, daughter of Charles Joel and Martha (Abernathy Herrin, as listed above, was born December 7, 1845, and died May 31, 1927. She married, at West Point, Tennessee, Josephus Sumter Johnson. He was born December 18, 1832, and died September 11, 1905. He was son of Robert and Mary (McLaren) Johnson. Robert Johnson lived at Columbia, in Maury County, Tennessee. He served in the War of 1812 as First Lieutenant, Captain Andrew McCarty's Company, First Regiment, West Tennessee Militia, commanded by Colonel Richard C. Napier. Enlisting in Maury County, January 28, 1814, he served until May 10, 1814. For his service, he received land in De Soto County,

Mississippi. Thence he moved to Wayland Springs, Lawrence County, Tennessee. He was killed there, by a horse, in 1836.

The children of Josephus Sumter and Amanda Fitzallen (Herrin) Johnson:

  i Richard Freeman Johnson; born September 16, 1864; married Mallie Springer, at West Point, Tennessee; resides at Midlothian, Texas; has children:

    1 Ruth Johnson; married Richard Newton, Midlothian, Texas; has children: Richard, Victor, Warren, Edith Ann, and Ruth Barker Newton.

    2 Mary Johnson.

    3 Rebecca Johnson; married C. K. Stark, Fort Worth, Texas; has children: Robert and Mary Bob Stark.

    4 Frank Johnson; married Nell ———, Long View, Texas; has son, Joseph Richard Johnson.

    5 Josephine Johnson; married Eldon Shiflett, Chicago, Illinois.

  ii Martha Ora Johnson; born May 9, 1866; died May 28, 1904; married Doctor Pressley, in Lawrence County, Tennessee; died in Texas; had daughter, Martha Ora Kelly, who married Frank Blair, Lawrenceburg, Tennessee.

  iii M. Lee Johnson; born January 5, 1868; is a physician; married Lula Luker, West Point, Tennessee; has children: Rachel, Marjorie, and Charles Johnson.

  iv Robert Charles Johnson; born March 4, 1870; married Saline Hardin, West Point, Tennessee; has child, Charlyne Johnson.

  v Lillie Johnson; born January 24, 1872; married Doctor George S. True, West Point, Tennessee; resides at Big Spring, Texas; has children:

    1 Mildred True; married Jerome Lusk, Big Spring, Texas; has children: Ruth Mildred, Joseph Martin, and Earl Jerome Lusk.

    2 Alline True; married, first, ——— Painter; second, ——— Scholte; third, John Williams, Dallas, Texas; has children: Mildred Painter and Charles Scholte.

LEEPER-DRAKE KITH AND KIN 49

    3 Archie True; married Myrtle ———, Big Spring, Texas.

    4 Georgia Earl True; married L. S. Ball; died, 1932, at Belen, New Mexico; had children: Helen Lucile, Lawrence Balland, and Bobbie Ball.

    5 Leta True; married R. H. Miller, Big Spring, Texas; has son, R. H. Miller, Junior.

    6 Valilia True; married Stanley Davis, Big Spring, Texas.

    7 Wanda True; married Hayden Griffith, Big Spring, Texas.

    8 Lucile True; married Fred Eugene Harrington; resides at Longview, Texas; has one child.

vi Edna Earl Johnson; born March 8, 1875; married, June 8, 1893, at Lewisburg, Tennessee, P. Marion Simms, born May 2, 1869; resides at Saint Edward, Nebraska; has children:

    1 Burney Gilmore Simms; born April 1, 1894; resides at Sacramento, California; married, at Vinton, Iowa, May 21, 1918, Merle Brown; children: Virginia, Frank Brown, and Thomas Johnson Simms.

    2 P. Marion Simms, Junior; born May 2, 1908.

vii Elbridge Herbert Johnson; born February 3, 1878; is a dentist; married Bessie Smith, Pine Bluff, Arkansas; has children: Mary Bess and Virginia Johnson.

viii Loulie Herrin Johnson; born October 6, 1880; resides at Russellville, Alabama; married W. F. Turner, West Point, Tennessee, now deceased; children:

    1 Judson Turner; died at age of about eighteen.

    2 Wilodine Turner; married Frank Hall, Lawrenceburg, Tennessee; has a son, William Hall, and an adopted daughter, Louise Hall.

    3 Frank Turner; married Doris ———, of Pine Bluff, Arkansas.

ix Mary Ella Johnson; born September 1, 1884; married, first, Joseph Belew, West Point, Tennessee; married, second, Harvey Couch, of West Point; has children:

      1 Robert Belew; married Nell ———, Lawrenceburg, Tennessee.
      2 James Belew; resides at Florence, Alabama; is married; has one child.
      3 Edith Belew; resides at Jasper, Alabama; married W. C. Inman; has four sons.
      4 William Couch.
  x Willie Sue Johnson; born May 9, 1887; married, first, William Welch, West Point, Tennessee; second, E. S. Howard, of Sylacauga, Alabama; has a son, William Welch, Junior.
  xi Emma Johnson; died in infancy.

Mastin C. Abernathy, the son of the above-described Freeman and Rachel (Drake) Abernathy, was brother to Martha Abernathy (wife of Charles Joel Herrin), whose descendants have now been noted, in the foregoing lineages. He was twice married, but the names of his wives are not known to the present compiler. His children, all but the first born of his second marriage, were:

  i Martha Ann Abernathy; married James Monroe Bryan, Lawrence County, Tennessee; had children:
      1 W. C. Bryan, of Fort Worth, Texas.
      2 Ina Bryan, of Fort Worth, Texas.
      3 Robert E. Bryan, of Shreveport, Louisiana.
      4 James A. Bryan; now deceased; had children, Nolan Bryan, of Fort Worth, and Ray Bryan, of Weatherford, Texas.
      5 Maude Bryan, of Fort Worth, Texas; married ——— Lott.
      6 Claude T. Bryan; now of United States Veterans Hospital, North Little Rock, Arkansas.
      7 Mattie M. Bryan, of Throckmorton, Texas; married ——— Franks.
  ii Thomas Abernathy.
  iii Freeman Abernathy, of Rotan, Texas.
  iv Laban Abernathy; now deceased; had two children.
  v Sallie Abernathy; married ——— Fry.
  vi ——— Abernathy, a daughter; of Stanton, Texas; married Joseph Kelly.

vii Mack Abernathy, of Big Spring, Texas.

Emily J. Abernathy was the daughter of Freeman and Rachel (Drake) Abernathy, aforesaid, and sister of the foregoing Martha and Mastin C. Abernathy, whose descendants have been mentioned herein. She married Robert C. Kelly. Their children were:

i Walter Kelly; had children:
    1 Woodie Gregory Kelly; had children: R. Walter Gregory Kelly, of Santa Monica, California; Edward Gregory Kelly; Willie Gregory Kelly, of Breckinridge, Texas; Albert Gregory Kelly, of Weatherford, Texas; Adel (Adele?) Gregory Kelly.
    2 Frederick Weatherford Kelly, of Eastland, Texas.
    3 Blunt Kelly, of Oklahoma.
    4 Scott Kelly, of Staunton, Texas.
    5 Benjamin Kelly.

ii James Kelly; had children:
    1 Jesse Kelly; deceased; his widow now residing in Pueblo, Colorado; had children: Della Kelly, who married ——— Foreman; Virginia Kelly, who married ——— MacDavis.
    2 Emma Kelly; resides at Mineral Wells, Texas; married ——— Pierce.
    3 Ella Kelly, of Mineral Wells; married ——— Hubbard.
    4 Katie Kelly, of Mineral Wells; married ——— Freeman.
    5 Earl Kelly, of Mineral Wells.

iii Mollie Kelly, of Hemet, California; married ——— Hall.

iv Martha Kelly; married ——— Hall; had children:
    1 Walter Hall, of Halley, Texas.
    2 Beulah Hall, of Weatherford, Texas; married ——— Carpenter.
    3 Robert Hall.
    4 Alma Hall.

  v Sallie Kelly; married ——— Hodges; had children:
    1 "Buddie" Hodges, of Yuma, Arizona.
    2 Cora Hodges.
    3 Richard Hodges.
    4 Guy Hodges.
    5 Aubry Hodges.
    6 Albert Hodges.
  vi "Bobbie" Kelly; married ——— Carr; had children:
    1 Bessie Carr; married ——— Walker.
    2 Myrtle Carr; married ——— Collier; resides at Midland, Texas.
    3 Nell Carr, of Weatherford, Texas; married ——— Jordan.
    4 Maude Carr; married ——— Howard.

Mary Abernathy, daughter of the aforesaid Freeman and Rachel (Drake) Abernathy (descendants of whose sisters, Martha and Emily J. Abernathy, and of whose brother, Mastin C. Abernathy, have now been listed herein), married Charles McLean. She had children:

  i Martha McLean; married ——— Hill.
  ii Nettie McLean; married ——— Crenshaw; had children:
    1 Charles Crenshaw.
    2 Minnie Crenshaw; married ——— Abernathy.
    3 Mabel Crenshaw; married ——— Glenn.
    4 Lizzie Crenshaw; married ——— Farris.
    5 James Crenshaw.
    6 Jane (or Jan) Crenshaw.
  iii Henrietta McLean; married ——— Sowell.

Jesse Logan Abernathy was the son of the aforesaid Freeman and Rachel (Drake) Abernathy. The descendants, as known, of his brothers and sisters have now been mentioned herein. He married, but the name of his wife is not known to the present compiler. He had children:

  i Mattie Abernathy, of Mineral Wells, Texas; married ——— Kelly.

ii Belle Abernathy, of Frederick, Oklahoma; married —— Carr.
iii Emma Abernathy; married —— Auburg.
iv Annie Abernathy; married —— Cook.

Albrittain Drake

IT HAS BEEN SHOWN above herein that the indications are very strong that Susan Drake, wife of Captain James Leeper, descended from Reverend Bamfield Drake. The latter's lineage, back to John Drake (who was grandfather of Sir Francis, the great Admiral), has been presented. It has also been stated herein that one Drake family, early in North Carolina, later in Kentucky, and other parts of the South, are known, by descendants, to have had this same Bamfield Drake for ancestor; and a quotation has been made from a letter, written in 1914, by a member of this line, declaring that Bible records and other proofs of this descent are extant.

According to the said letter, Albrittain Drake, born in Devonshire, was son of James Drake. James was son of Francis and Mary (Buckingham) Drake; and this Francis was son of the aforesaid Reverend Bamfield Drake.

Miss Kate Drake, of Gibson, Mississippi, a descendant of this branch of the family, states that James, father of Albrittain, was born in 1725, and died in 1790. James Drake came to America, and lived in Nash County, North Carolina. During the War of the Revolution, Captain Beard, evidently either an English soldier, or an American fighting on the side of the English, attacked the house of James Drake, with a band of Tories. James and his son, Albrittain Drake, and half-a-dozen other men were the only defenders. Albrittain was a soldier in the American forces, and then a member of a corps of Light Horse, which had been on active duty, scouring the countryside for this same band of Tories under Captain Beard. Outnumbering the Drakes and their companions, the enemy demanded surrender. James Drake, seizing a gun, rushed at the Tories, firing, but missed his mark, as did also his opponent. The latter's shot, however, wounded several other of the defenders. Beard, entering the house, sword in hand, met young Albrittain Drake, armed with a cutlass. This weapon, with its first blow, struck the joist above its wielder's head, was broken off at the hilt, and he struck down. The father, armed with a club, flew to Albrittain's defense, but fell beneath Beard's sword-thrusts, so badly wounded that he was "a gore of blood," as the story has come down. According to the tradition, James Drake's wife, seeing her husband thus overcome, and her son also struck down, rushed in, armed with a jug of what was known as "Old Nash" brandy. Whether she used this as an external weapon, history saith not; but, with it, she induced the enemy to pause for parley, and peace seemed restored. Just then, however, the American Captain Peter Goodwin galloped up with a troop of Horse, and Beard and the Tories were driven off.

Albrittain Drake, son of James Drake, was born in 1755, according to Wheeler's History of North Carolina, which states that he was eighty when he died, the year of his death, 1835, being given in his War Record, from the Bureau of Pensions, at Washington. This record, however, gives his birth-year as 1760, rather than 1755, and the place of his birth as Edgecombe County, North Carolina, rather than Devonshire, England, mentioned, as above stated, by one of his descendants.

When he enlisted to fight for American liberty, he was a resident of Nash County, North Carolina. This was in October, 1777. He served then for three months, as a Private in Captain Hardy's Company, Colonel Long's Regiment. He became a Lieutenant by January, 1778, when he re-enlisted, and served, with that rank, till the autumn of 1782. He removed to Kentucky, where he was living in Muhlenburg County when, September 29, 1832, he applied for a Revolutionary pension, which was granted to him. He died on November 14, 1835.

About 1785, Albrittain Drake married Ruth Collins. She was born November 12, 1765, and died March 4, 1847. The children of Albrittain and Ruth (Collins) Drake were as follows:

i John Drake; born May 26, 1786. (See, below, "A Lineage from John Drake.")
ii Sophia (or Sophia Valentine) Drake; born January 5, 1789; married Wiley Alford.
iii Silas Drake; born November 4, 1791.
iv Mosley Collins Drake; born May 5, 1795.
v Perry Drake; born September 15, 1797.*
vi Benjamin Michael Drake; described subsequently.
vii William Drake; born December 14, 1804. (See, below, "Drake and Bridgers Items.")
viii Edmund Drake; born May 21, 1807.

The names and birth-dates of these children appear in the aforementioned Revolutionary Record of Albrittain Drake, their father,

---

*He was Colonel of 1st Indiana Volunteers in the Mexican War, and his name, as recorded in the Pension Office, was James Perry Drake. He died, 1876, at Huntsville, Alabama. His wife was Priscilla Holmes.

in the Bureau of Pensions, at Washington. Miss Kate Drake, of Fort Gibson, Mississippi, stated that Sophia, one of these children, and the only daughter of Albrittain Drake, married Wiley Alford.

Benjamin Michael Drake, son of Albrittain and Ruth (Collins) Drake, was born, as in his father's Revolutionary Record, on September 11, 1800. He died in 1860. In 1827, Benjamin Michael Drake married Susan, daughter of James Trueman Magruder. They had a son, Elijah Steel Drake.

Elijah Steel Drake, son of Benjamin Michael and Susan (Magruder) Drake, was born in 1841, and died in 1914. He was one of twelve children of his parents. His father had moved from Kentucky to Mississippi, and became a Methodist preacher. In 1869, Elijah Steel Drake (whose middle name is also spelled Steele in records received), married Ellen Davis Turpin.

Elijah Steel and Ellen Davis (Turpin) Drake had two sons and four daughters. The sons were Joseph T. Drake, a lawyer, and H. W. M. Drake. One of the daughters is Miss Kate Drake, of Fort Gibson, Mississippi, who supplied the data on this lineage in great part.

A Lineage from John Drake, Eldest Son of Albrittain Drake

JOHN DRAKE, as noted above, was born May 26, 1786, the first-born child of Albrittain and Ruth (Collins) Drake. He married Elizabeth Alford.

Zachariah Drake, son of John and Elizabeth (Alford) Drake, also married an Alford,—as had, likewise, Sophia Drake, only daughter of the aforesaid Albrittain Drake. Her husband was Wiley Alford. As the wife of Zachariah Drake was Sophia Alford, it seems probable that she was daughter to the said Wiley and Sophia (Drake) Alford. In this case, she was first cousin to Zachariah Drake.

Agenora Drake was the daughter of Zachariah and Sophia (Alford) Drake. She married James Peterkin.

Elizabeth Peterkin, daughter of James and Agenora (Drake) Peterkin, was born in Marlboro County, South Carolina. She married Robert Adams. Mrs. Adams entered the society of Daughters of the American Revolution, as a descendant of Albrittain Drake, record of whose service as a patriot has already been set forth herein.

Drake and Bridgers Items

MENTION HAS BEEN MADE already of a letter, written in 1914 (whence and to whom unknown to the present compiler), concerning Albrittain Drake, his father, James Drake, and their lineage back to Thomas Drake, youngest brother of Sir Francis Drake, the great Admiral. The still earlier ancestry, to John Drake, grandfather of the Admiral and of the said Thomas Drake, has been presented herein. This letter of 1914 gives the following additional data concerning James and Albrittain Drake and their branch of the family.

The letter was evidently written by John R. Drake, his place of residence not mentioned. He was son of William Drake, who was son of Albrittain Drake, as stated above.

James Drake, father of Albrittain Drake, married twice, states Mr. John R. Drake, in the said letter. His first wife was Sophia Valentine. As already mentioned herein, Albrittain Drake, son of James, named his daughter Sophia, or Sophia Valentine,—evidently for her grandmother. The second wife of James Drake, says Mr. John R. Drake, was a widow, Mrs. Davis, who had one son by her former marriage.

As has already been described herein, James Drake, father of Albrittain, was son of Francis and Mary (Buckingham) Drake. Mr. John R. Drake says that this Francis Drake married, second, a widow, Mrs. Bridgers; that she had, by her first marriage, a son, Samuel Bridgers; and that he thinks this Samuel Bridgers married Sallie Drake, "the sister of my grandfather Big Albrittain."

Apparently,—judging from this letter of Mr. John R. Drake,—this Samuel (also called "Sampson") Bridgers and Sallie Drake, his wife, had children as follows:

    i Hearty Bridgers; married John Brittain Drake, whose place in the family-tree is not mentioned by Mr. John R. Drake.

    ii "Little Brittain Drake Clopton of Columbia, Tennessee," as named by Mr. John R. Drake in his said letter, but who, supposedly, bore the surname of Bridgers.

    iii Penelope Bridgers, "who married Richard Drake (a brother of Little Brittain) and father of James William Drake of Pontotoc, Miss. (who was grandfather to my wife Heonia Carr.)"

It is impossible to state exactly, from the transcript of Mr. John R. Drake's letter available to the present compiler; but it seems probable that the above-noted "Little Brittain Drake Clopton of Columbia, Tennessee," was recorded incorrectly in the said transcript; and that Samuel and Sallie (Drake) Bridgers had but two children, the two daughters mentioned,—Hearty and Penelope.

The husbands of these daughters,—both Drakes,—belonged, as will be described subsequently herein, to the family descending from Richard Drake, who was brother to James Drake, and, therefore, was uncle to Albrittain Drake.

As will also be seen, the above-mentioned Sallie, or Sarah Drake, daughter of James and sister of Albrittain, who, says Mr. John R. Drake, married Samuel Bridgers, as he thinks, is given a different husband in records of the lineage from Richard.

The present compiler has a transcript of another letter, written in Pontotoc, Mississippi, August 5, 1857. It begins, "Dear Jack," and ends, "Your Cousin James." The writer evidently belonged to the said branch descending from Richard Drake, brother of James, and uncle of Albrittain. This letter says: "I learned that our grandfather Bridgers descended from a widow Drake . . . who had a son from whom descended old Major John Drake. . . . That widow Drake after she became a widow married Bridgers from whom descended our grandfather William Bridgers and his several brothers."

Descendants of Richard Drake

RICHARD DRAKE, as already said, was brother to James Drake, whose descendants, through his son, Albrittain Drake, have herein been recorded. It is said that Richard and James came from England to Virginia, that James went on to North Carolina, and that Richard lived at Southampton, Virginia. This probably means in Southampton County. The date of their coming to America is not known, but, as already mentioned herein, James is believed to have been born in 1725. Southampton County was formed, in 1749, from Isle of Wight and Nansemond Counties.

Richard Drake died between February 28, 1759, and September 13, 1759, the dates when his Will was made and proved, in Southampton County. In this document, he mentioned the following: his sons, Nathaniel, Tristram,* William (mentioned as married to Zilpah Kirby), Brittain (or Brittian), Richard,—to whom most of his father's lands were bequeathed,—and Edmund; his daughter, "Martha Williams, the wife of Jacob Williams"; apparently, other daughters, Elizabeth and Margaret. The transcript of the Will furnished the present compiler, however, does not seem to be an exact copy, and, from other sources, it appears that he had but one daughter, besides the said Martha, namely, a daughter, Margaret, known as Peggy. The Will, in the transcript, at least, does not mention sons, Matthew and Francis; but they are stated, in other sources, to have been sons of this Richard Drake.

So far as can be determined, it is probable that the following is a correct list of Richard Drake's children, though the order of their births is unknown.

    i Matthew Drake; described subsequently.
    ii Francis Drake; settled in Chatham County, North Carolina.
    iii William Drake; described subsequently.
    iv Nathaniel Drake; described subsequently.
    v Tristram Drake; described subsequently.
    vi Richard Drake; settled in Chatham County, North Carolina.
    vii Edmund Drake; described subsequently.

---

*This name is spelled variously in records furnished for the present compilation. The form, Tristram, has been followed herein, as seeming most probably correct to the compiler. Possibly, however, the name was Thruston.

viii Martha Drake; married Jacob Williams; had children:
   1 John Williams.
   2 James Williams.
   3 Jerry Williams.
   4 Matthew Williams.
   5 Polly Williams.
   6 "Patsy" Williams.
   7 Nancy Williams.
ix Margaret Drake; married Edmund Branch; had no children.

Matthew Drake, son of Richard Drake, settled in Nash County, then part of Edgecombe County, North Carolina. He was Justice of the Peace of that County in 1782. He espoused the cause of the patriots in the War for American Independence, and served this cause in his public activities.

When the new County of Nash was erected in 1777, the General Assembly of North Carolina appointed him as member of a committee concerned with construction of the public buildings of the County.* He died in or by 1810, when his Will was proved in Nash County.

Matthew Drake married Ann Arrington, and they had the following children:

i Matthew Drake, Junior; married Milly, daughter of General Hardy Griffin.
ii James Drake; married ———, daughter of Peter Arrington.
iii Mourning Drake; married Caswell Drake, son of Edmund Drake, the last being son of Richard Drake aforesaid brother to James Drake, and first American ancestor of the Drake line now being described herein.
iv "Patsy" Drake (Martha?); married, first, William Parker; second, ——— Woodruff.
v Betsy Drake; married Michael Collins.
vi Polly Drake; married Duke W. Sumner; described below.

---

*Other members of this commttee were Duncan Lamon, Nathan Boddie, Edward Clinch, and Arthur Arrington.

vii Frank Drake; perhaps older than his brother, James, above mentioned; married Betsy Drake, daughter of William Drake, son of Richard, ancestor of this branch of the Drake family in America.

viii "Tempy" Drake; married Exum (?) P. Sumner.

ix "Dolly" Drake; married, first, John Sumner; second, Judge ——— Phillips.

x Amy Drake; died, aged twelve years.

Mary Drake, often referred to as "Polly," and thus named in the foregoing list of children of Matthew and Ann (Arrington) Drake, —said Matthew being, as already stated, son of Richard, ancestor of this line,—was born November 27, 1779, and died in June, 1813. About 1799, she married Duke W. Sumner, mentioned above. He was born April 27, 1778, and died May 5, 1844.

Temperance Ann Sumner was the daughter of the said, Duke W. and Mary (Drake) Sumner. She was born September 16, 1812, and died November 23, 1899. She married, January 13, 1831, John Bass. He was born in November, 1793, and died May 19, 1860.

Mary Bass, daughter of John and Temperance Ann (Sumner) Bass, was born December 8, 1832, and died March 12, 1858. On December 12, 1849, she married Jacob Sumner. He was born in June, 1822, and died January 28, 1872.

Laura Sumner was the daughter of Jacob and Mary (Bass) Sumner. She was born March 24, 1852, and died March 22, 1892. On May 15, 1874, she married Mosley Stratton. He was born August 17, 1845, and died July 14, 1910.

Nina Stratton, daughter of Mosley and Laura (Sumner) Stratton, married Edgar M. Foster. She became a member of the Daughters of the American Revolution, through her descent from Matthew Drake, whose Revolutionary service has been described above herein.

Edgar M. and Nina (Stratton) Foster had one child, Mosley Stratton Foster, who married November 9, 1938, Miss Eleanor Inman Gray, daughter of Mr. and Mrs. Walker Inman Gray of Atlanta, Georgia.

William Drake, son of Richard, American progenitor of this branch of the Drake family, settled in Edgecombe County, now Nash County, North Carolina. He married Zilpah Kirby. She was a sister of William Kirby, who married Sarah Drake, daughter of

James Drake, the last being a brother of Richard, ancestor of the Drake line now being described herein.

Information as to this Kirby and Drake connection was given by Mrs. John Lewis Kirby, who was formerly Miss Elizabeth White. She is the great-granddaughter of William and Sarah (Drake) Kirby aforesaid, and her husband descended from the same Kirby family. He was a son of John Lewis Kirby, and was born in Nashville, Tennessee. He was one of the most widely known men connected with the religious Press in the South. In 1859 and 1860, he became associated with *The Gallatin Examiner*. Afterwards, he was City Editor of *The Nashville Dispatch*. His work on the last paper won recognition, and he became connected with *The Louisville Courier-Journal,* having George D. Prentice and Henry Watterson as co-workers. After the Civil War, he took a post with the Methodist Publishing House of Nashville, Tennessee, directing in an editorial capacity several church publications. Eventually, he took charge of the Sunday School publications, and continued in this service until a few months before his death.

John Lewis Kirby and Elizabeth White of Sumner County, Tennessee, were married October 1, 1867. Mrs. Kirby now lives in Coral Gables, Florida. Their children are:

i Lula Kirby; now a resident of Florida; married John Hone, of New York.

ii Bessie Kirby; married ——— Adams; had several children; one daughter, Marion Adams.

iii Leon D. Kirby; of Sewanee, Tennessee.

Returning to the description of the aforesaid William Drake, husband of Zilpah Kirby, their children are listed as follows:

i Matthew Drake; died unmarried.

ii William Drake; died unmarried.

iii Brittain Drake; married a daughter of William Bridgers.*

iv Richard Drake; married another daughter of William Bridgers.*

v John Drake; married Chloe, daughter of George Boddie.

---

*See, above, under "Drake and Bridgers Items." Statements therein made, based on information deduced from transcript of a letter, written, 1914, by John R. Drake, give Hearty Bridgers, wife of *Samuel* Bridgers (rather than William Bridgers), as wife of "John Brittain Drake;" and also give Penelope Bridgers (named as daughter of *Samuel* Bridgers), as wife of "Richard Drake (a brother of Little Brittain)."

    vi Sallie Drake; died in young girlhood, unmarried.

    vii Betsy Drake; married Frank Drake, son of Matthew Drake (Matthew Drake, described above, being brother to William Drake, father of this Betsy), as has already been stated, above herein.

Nathaniel Drake (called in records of the family, "Natt"), was son of the aforesaid Richard Drake, American ancestor of this branch of the family. He settled in the northern part of what then was Edgecombe County, now Nash County, North Carolina. He married Delilah Floyd, and they had the following children:

    i Orrin Drake; died unmarried.
    ii Dyer Drake; married ———, daughter of Jerry Williams.
    iii Paliman Drake; died young.
    iv "Natt" Drake; died unmarried.
    v Allen Drake; died young.
    vi Betsy Drake; married Gilford Griffin, son of General Hardy Griffin.
    vii Peggy Drake; died unmarried.
    viii ——— Drake; a daughter; whose name and history is unknown.

Tristram Drake was another son of Richard Drake, first American ancestor of this branch of the family. He settled in Halifax County, North Carolina. He married, but his wife's name is not known. They had sons:

    i Eli Drake.
    ii Richard Drake; married Louisa ("Louicy") Drake, who was daughter of Edmund Drake, brother of Tristram Drake, aforesaid.
    iii Tristram Drake, Junior.
    iv Herbert Drake.
    v Jesse Francis Drake; had a son, Elias Drake.

Edmund Drake, brother of the foregoing Tristram Drake, and, thus, son of Richard, first American ancestor of this line, is said to have settled in what became West Virginia. He married Polly Mann, daughter of Thomas and Betsy Mann, and they had children:

    i Edwin Drake; died unmarried.
    ii Augustine Drake; died unmarried.

- iii Henry Drake; married ———, daughter of Henry Vaux.
- iv Caswell Drake; married Mourning Drake, daughter of Matthew Drake (brother of Edmund Drake, whose children are now listed), as has been mentioned, above herein.
- v Chloe Drake; married Lemuel Nicholson.
- vi Louisa Drake; married Richard Drake, son of Tristram Drake (son of Richard, and brother of Edmund Drake, now described), as already mentioned.
- vii Lizzie Drake; married James Green.
- viii Polly Drake; married, first, William Dozier; second, James Screws.
- ix Penelope ("Penny") Drake; married Henry Mitchell.
- x "Patsy" Drake; married Richmond Dozier.
- xi Sally Drake; married, first, Richard Olive; second, ——— Montgomery.
- xii Nancy Drake.

Descendants of Captain John Drake, of Philadelphia, Pennsylvania, and Huntsville, Alabama

THERE APPEARS no connection, in America, between the ancestral lineage, or the kinsfolk, of Susan Drake, wife of Captain James Leeper, and the family now to be studied; but it is possible that this last was also descended from the family in England to which belonged Sir Francis Drake, the great Admiral, or, it may be, from Drakes of some ancestral connection with this branch.

Captain John Drake was born, at a place unknown, in 1749. He died in 1840, aged ninety. He resided in Philadelphia, Pennsylvania, is said to have gone thence to "the Carolinas," and settled in Huntsville, Alabama, about 1800. There has also been made a statement that he belonged to the Drake family of New Jersey. He is believed to have been a soldier in the War of the Revolution, and it may be that it was because of this service that he received, from the Government, a tract of one thousand acres, in Alabama. To this he appears to have added eight hundred more acres. A descendant writes: "He said that he was going to build the finest house in the County. I remember as a child having seen a dark red or black silk quilt on which was embroidered the design of the house, with the figures of the members of the family in the foreground, and, in the rear, the figures of the faithful slaves. This was owned by Mrs. Amanda Bright."

Captain Drake had a sister, Elizabeth Drake, and they belonged to the Society of Friends, or Quakers. If he was a soldier, he must have been somewhat at variance with the other members of the sect, but many Quakers have forgotten their tenet of pacifism when patriotism called. His wife's Christian name is unknown, but her surname was Neeley. They were married before leaving the North. After her death, Captain Drake returned to Philadelphia, and there he died. Their children were:

    i Neeley Drake; settled in Mississippi; born 1798; died 1876.

    ii James F. (probably Franklin) Drake; described subsequently.

    iii Andrew Drake; settled near Huntsville, Alabama.

    iv Eliza Drake; lived at Big Cove, the State not mentioned in records gathered.

v   Zachariah Drake; thought to have been perhaps named, in full, Zachariah Charles, or Charles Zachariah, though it may be that their two sons, Zachariah and Charles; "Charles Drake" settling in East Tennessee.

vi   William Drake; settled at Russellville, Alabama.

vii   Anne Drake.

viii   Sarah Jane Drake.

James Franklin Drake, as his full name probably was, son of Captain John and ――― (Neeley) Drake, settled at Little Cove, whose State is not mentioned in the records gathered. He was twice married. His first wife was his second cousin, on the maternal side of the family, Rose Anne Neeley. He married, second, Mary, daughter of Captain James Bright, of Fayette, Tennessee. This is as stated in records gathered; but a conflicting statement, in the same records, declares that he married, second, in 1816, Agnes Neeley,—doubtless, also, a relative, through his mother. This last is probably correct, and it was his son, of the same name, who married Mary Bright, as will be noted below.

The children of James Franklin Drake, by his said second marriage, to Agnes Neeley, were all daughters, whose names are unknown. They are said to have married members of the Drake family.

The children of James Franklin and Rose Anne (Neeley) Drake were:

i   Evelyn, or Evelina, Drake; described subsequently.

ii   Julia Drake; married John Reese.

iii   John Robin Drake; married, first, Agnes Shannon; second, ――― Termant; had a son, Horace Drake.

iv   James Franklin Drake, Junior; described subsequently.

Evelyn, or Evelina Drake, both names being used in records of her, was born September 5, 1808. She died May 12, 1872. She married Berry Leftwich Stone, known as "Little Berry Leftwich Stone," probably son of a man of the same name, "Little" being sometimes used in parts of the South in place of the more common term, "Junior." They were married May 21, 1830.

Berry ("Little Berry") Leftwich and Evelyn (Drake) Stone had a son and five daughters, the names of the daughters being unknown. The son was James Stone. James Stone married, and had a daughter, Julia Stone, who married James A. Yowell. She is deceased, and was buried in Lone Oak Cemetery, Lewisburg, Tennessee. She and her husband, who survives her, had a son, Joseph Yowell, who is married and has five children. Mrs. Yowell had two sisters: ———— Stone, who married Tillman Lamb, of Memphis, Tennessee; ———— Stone, who married Iverson Rodes, of Nashville, Tennessee.

James Franklin Drake, Junior, son of James Franklin and Rose Anne (Neeley) Drake, married, first, Mary Bright, daughter of Captain James Bright, of Fayette, Tennessee. She was born in October, 1837, and died in 1854. James Franklin Drake, Junior, married, second, in 1855, Nancy Morgan.

Children of James Franklin Drake, Junior, and his first wife, Mary Bright, were:

 i James Bright Drake; married Mattie McEwen.

 ii Edwin Lucius Drake; described subsequently.

The records of this especial family, as well as those of descendants of Edwin Lucius Drake, just mentioned, are in much confusion, and it is very probable, therefore, that some items really belonging here, must be omitted. In the record sent, listing the two above-named sons of James Franklin Drake, Junior, there follows this:

> "Sallie Smith
>
> Blanchard Drake Smith.
>
> The above family was reared at Lagrange, where their grandfather Smith was president of the Lagrange Female College, where their father E. B. S. taught also."

Possibly this means that Sallie Drake was daughter of James Franklin Drake, Junior; that she married E. B. Smith; that she had a son, Blanchard Drake Smith (and, assumably, other children, from the use of the word, "family," in the above quotation); and that her husband's father was President of the said College.

Edwin Lucius Drake, son of James Franklin Drake, Junior, and his wife, Mary Bright, was a physician. He married, first, 1867, in Sumner County, Tennessee, Mary Blanche Branham. It seems possible to the present compiler that her surname was really Smith, and that Branham was her middle name; for her children are recorded as "Paul Smith" (Drake?) and "Yula May Smith, married Jesse Cater, Lagrange, Georgia." The mention of Lagrange Female College, in the quotation made above, seems to add to the puzzle.

It seems to the present compiler that the actual facts were as follows: that Mary Blanche Drake, recorded as daughter of Doctor Edwin Lucius and Mary Blanche (Branham) Drake, married Earl B. Smith (noted, doubtless, in error, as "Earler S. Smith," but who appears to have been the "E. B. S." mentioned in the above quotation). She was married in Texas, but he was from Lagrange, Georgia. It may be that Mary Blanche Drake, who married Earl B. Smith, died early, and that, because of this, her family was brought up in the home, at Lagrange, Georgia, of their grandfather, ——— Smith, President of Lagrange Female College, where, also, their father, Earl B. Smith ("E. B. S." in the quotation), taught.

Mary Blanche (Branham) Drake, wife of Doctor Edwin Lucius Drake, died in 1869. On December 5, 1876, Doctor Drake married, second, Nina Louisana Duffield, at Winchester, Tennessee. The children of this marriage appear to have been as follows:

 i Elizabeth Bright Drake; born at Fayetteville, Tennessee, October 7, 1877.

 ii Edwin Franklin Drake; born November 23, 1878; died in infancy.

 iii Eloise Morgan Drake; described subsequently.

 iv Franklin Duffield Drake; born in 1883, at Collinsville, Texas.

 v Marguerite Lewis Drake; born October 19, 1885, at Sherman, Texas; was twice married, but names of her husbands are unknown to the present compiler.*

 vi Lucia Roberta Drake; born August 31, 1887, at Winchester, Tennessee; died June 13, 1931.

 vii Douglas Martin Drake; married Betty Gordon Lane, of Pulaski, Tennessee.

 viii John Polk Drake; married Emma Walker.

 ix Charles Neeley Drake; married Frances Richardson, Paris, Texas.

 x Ella Maria Drake; married Doctor ——— Whitten, of Virginia and Texas.

Eloise Morgan Drake, daughter, as above mentioned, of Doctor Edwin Lucius and Nina Louisana (Duffield) Drake, was born at Winchester, Tennessee, August 22, 1880. On December 5, 1903,

---

*Perhaps they were: first, Mark Lohnen, of Nashville, Tennessee, married and died, 1927; second, 1931, J. R. Morgan, of Hamlet, North Carolina.

at Winchester, she married R. C. Bannerman, who was born in 1875, at Pigeon Cove, Massachusetts.

The children of R. C. and Eloise Morgan (Drake) Bannerman:

    i Louise Morgan Bannerman; born at Huntsville, Alabama, November 19, 1904; married Dena Young, June 2, 1930, Washington, D. C.

    ii Catherine Thackeray Bannerman; born October 2, 1906, at Decatur, Georgia.

    iii Christine Elizabeth Bannerman; born May 15, 1908, at Decatur, Georgia; married William Werner Bradford, November 2, 1929, at Frederick, Maryland.

    iv Robert Lee Bannerman; born March 11, 1916, at Red Granite, Mississippi.

    v Mary Lucia Bannerman; born at Winnipeg, Manitoba, Canada.

Smith and Descended Families

SARAH JANE LEEPER, the only child of Captain James Leeper and Susan Drake, his wife, married, at the age of seventeen, on November 22, 1798, Alexander Smith. She was born October 25, 1781, and died November 19, 1866. Her husband was born May 17, 1769, and died July 22, 1840.

Alexander Smith was the son of Robert and Sarah Y. (Clemmons) Smith. There is strong reason to think that this Smith family was of Cumberland County, Virginia. This is discussed subsequently herein, under the history of the Criddle family. By the late 1780's, however, Robert Smith had become a land-owner, and, probably, a resident, of North Carolina. On July 10, 1788, he received, from the State of North Carolina, a Grant of five thousand acres, "lying and being in our middle District lying on Duck river about four miles above the mouth of Sugar Creek." On December 6, 1794, he received two other Grants. One of these was for six hundred and forty acres, "in our middle District lying on the north fork of Duck river in Wilson's valley between the head of Caring Spring Creek and big Harpeth." The other tract was two thousand acres, "in our middle District on the North side of the North fork of Duck river in Wilson's valley."

Robert Smith's wife, Sarah Y. Clemmons, was the daughter of John and Mary Clemmons. She was born February 7, 1728, and died February 8, 1809. Her resting-place is in the Hightower cemetery, on the Wilson Pike, at Brentwood, Tennessee, and her stone is the oldest there. The known children of Robert and Sarah Y. (Clemmons) Smith were the following:

 i Elizabeth Smith; described under Criddle family history.

 ii Sarah Smith; described under Ewing family history.

 iii Alexander Smith; further described subsequently.

 iv Nancy L. Smith; described presently.

Nancy L. Smith, just-mentioned daughter of Robert and Sarah Y. (Clemmons), Smith, was born February 13, 1770. One record gives her death-date as June 6, 1826; while another states that it was June 6, 1819.

On October 17, 1791, she married Richard Hightower. He was born May 25, 1761, and died October 11, 1820. The Hightower home was at Brentwood, Tennessee, on the Wilson Pike.

It is not known to the present compiler whether Richard and Nancy L. (Smith) Hightower had other children, but they had these following:

    i Mary S. Hightower; born in January, 1802; died May 7, 1833; married William Hadley.

    ii Joseph B. Hightower; born February 9, 1804; died July 20, 1834.

    iii Sarah Clemmons Hightower; described presently.

    iv Hardy Hightower; perhaps son of Richard and Nancy L. (Smith) Hightower, as his daughter, mentioned below, was buried in the cemetery on Richard Hightower's estate; married Harriet ———; had a daughter: Harriet M. Hightower, born January 28, 1820, died February 17, 1834, buried, as said, on Richard Hightower's estate, at Brentwood, Tennessee; said Hardy Hightower and his wife, Harriet M., residing in Lauderdale County, Alabama.

Sarah Clemmons Hightower, daughter of Richard and Nancy L. (Smith) Hightower, married Oliver Bliss Hayes, a prominent citizen of Nashville, Tennessee. Their first home, after their marriage, was near the site of the present Hermitage Hotel, in Nashville. Later, they purchased Rokeby, then a country estate, and it remained for many years in the possession of the family. Mr. Hayes was a lawyer, but, in later life, he became a Presbyterian Minister. Being a man of large means, he gave his services without price, and thus it came about that many Nashville people whose means were small went to Rokeby to have the beloved divine perform their marriage ceremonies, since he asked no fee. The Hayes family property holdings included a large section of West End, and Hayes, Acklen, Addison, Boyd, Adelicia, Laura, and Corinna were seven of Nashville's thoroughfares which perpetuated the name of this family, its members, and connections. They had much to do with the upbuilding of Nashville. Some of these streets and avenues still bear these names. The homes of this family and its connections were among the handsomest in the city, and several of them are still standing.

The children, as known to the compiler, or indicated as children, of Oliver Bliss and Sarah Clemmons (Hightower) Hayes:

 i Henry M. Hayes; lived in the fine old residence, now the Nurses' Home of St. Thomas' Hospital, at Nashville; married Leonora Boyd; had a daughter, ——— Hayes, who married Henry W. Forde.

 ii Adelicia Hayes; described below.

 iii Richard H. Hayes; born in 1813; died December 4, 1838; buried in the Hightower Cemetery at Brentwood, Tennessee.

 iv Corinna Hayes; born in 1819; died in 1821; buried in the Hightower Cemetery aforesaid.

 v Oliver Bliss Hayes, Junior; born December 20, 1824; date of death unknown, but was buried in the Hightower Cemetery.

 vi Aurelia Hayes; born September 5, the year not known; died October 25, 1850; buried in the Hightower Cemetery.

Adelicia Hayes, daughter of the above-described Oliver Bliss and Sarah Clemmons (Hightower) Hayes, spent her young girlhood at Rokeby, the home, as already mentioned, of her parents. She married, first, Isaac Franklin, who was a wealthy planter. As a lovely young widow, she married Joseph Acklen. In 1850, Mr. and Mrs. Acklen built for their home Belmont, said at that time to be the handsomest private establishment in the United States. This stately structure is, today, the Ward-Belmont College for girls and women, which, for more than sixty years, has occupied a high position in the social and educational facilities of the nation. Together with its opportunities for culture in literature and art, this institution has preserved and fostered traditions of the Old South in the days of crinoline, and has received students from the finest homes throughout the country.

In "Queens of American Society," by Mrs. Ellet, published in 1867, by Charles Scribner and Company, there is an elaborate and illustrated biographical sketch of Adelicia (Hayes) Acklen. It relates that, after the death of Mr. Acklen, she, with her children, spent two years in Europe, and mentions her attendance at the Imperial Ball, given at the opening of the French National Assembly by the Emperor Napoleon III and the Empress Eugenie, who received her "with marked consideration." "Her beauty, graces and courtly manners, with her rich, tasteful dress at all times and the superb style in which she lived, created a sensation in Paris and in social circles. She was universally admired." The book describes with admiration her home at Belmont, to whose adornment she brought from Europe many additions,—paintings, sculpture, engravings, exquisite articles of *vertu*. It says: "She is no less distinguished for her generous charities than for her brilliant social graces. Hers is the home of cordial hospitality, to which resort all the celebrities who visit Nashville, and the poor partake of the profuse liberality that marks entertainments."

Mrs. Acklen married, third, Doctor William A. Cheatham.

Mention has now been made of the descendants, so far as known to the compiler, of Nancy L. Smith, daughter of Robert and Sarah Y. (Clemmons) Smith, and sister of Alexander Smith. The last-named was the husband of Sarah Jane Leeper, only child of Captain James Leeper and Susan Drake, his wife.

Alexander Smith, as already noted, was born May 17, 1769. After his marriage to Sarah Jane Leeper, on November 22, 1798, they went to live on the rich, fertile land in the Little Harpeth Valley, in Williamson County, Tennessee, which had been granted to Captain Leeper for his military service.

He was a surveyor, an important occupation in the pioneer days, and was one of the three Commissioners appointed by Tennessee to settle the boundary line between that State and North Carolina. The other two Tennessee Commissioners were Isaac Allen and Simeon Perry, and the three North Carolina Commissioners were James Mebane, Montfort Stokes, and Robert Love. The six men made report "To His Excellency Joseph McMinn, Governor of the State of Tennessee," in a document, "Given under our hands at Knoxville in the State of Tennessee on the 31st day of August 1821." They stated that they had "met at the town of Newport in the State of Tennessee on the 16th day of July A. D. 1821 to settle, run and mark the dividing line between the two states from the termination of the line run by McDowell, Vance and Matthews in the year of our Lord 1799, to the Southern boundary of the said States." They then proceeded, in the Report, to describe in detail the line of boundary which they had marked.

On May 12, 1807, Alexander Smith was a party in an agreement concerning the surveying and granting of land in Tennessee. An abstract of this follows.

"Memorandum of an agreement made this the 12th day of May in the year 1807, between William T. Lewis of the one part and James

Robertson, Henry Rutherford, Richard Hightower and Alexander Smith of the other part. Witnesseth that the said William T. Lewis hath agreed to furnish and deliver to the said James Robertson, Henry Rutherford, Richard Hightower and Alexander Smith on or before the first day of August next, warrants or certificates issued by the Commissioners of West Tennessee agreeable to an Act of the General Assembly entitled an Act Directing the Division of the State into convenient Districts, etc., passed the 12th day of September last, to the amount of thirty thousand acres or more: and the said James Robertson, Henry Rutherford, Richard Hightower and Alexander Smith . . . do hereby covenant and agree to and with the said William T. Lewis, . . . that they will at some time before the first day of April next, cause said certificates to be located on vacant and unappropriated lands within the first, second or third Districts laid off by said act . . . also procure entries thereof to be made in the surveyors office . . . and also that they will . . . procure such lands to be correctly surveyed and grants thereof to be finally completed to the said William T. Lewis,................ the said William T. Lewis, . . . doth thereupon covenant and agree to and with the said James Robertson, Henry Rutherford, Richard Hightower and Alexander Smith, their heirs and assigns, by a good and lawful deed or deeds of conveyance in fee simple first part of such lands founded on locations heretofore made, and one half of such lands to be obtained by virtue of locations hereafter to be made, . . . and to prevent all doubts as to the . . . meaning of this latter covenant it is further expressed as the true intent and meaning thereof that said William T. Lewis is to retain in case of a division into three parts two-thirds and in other cases one half of each tract . . ."

This agreement was ordered to be recorded, by the Clerk of Davidson County, Tennessee, Nathan Ewing, at the April Session of the County Court, in 1813.

The home of Alexander and Sarah Jane (Leeper) Smith was at Brentwood, already noted herein as the home of Richard Hightower and his wife, Nancy L. Smith, the sister of Alexander Smith. Richard Hightower, as stated, was associated with Alexander Smith, in the above-quoted memorandum of agreement with William T. Lewis. Brentwood is now a station beautifully situated on the Louisville and Nashville Railroad, in Williamson County, near the boundary line between that County and Davidson County. The railroad now runs through the Smith estate. Alexander Smith and his wife spent long, useful years there, improving it constantly. Eventually, they built, on their land, a meal and flour mill and a furniture factory. Thenceforth, they had the generous pleasure of distributing largesse to their less fortunate neighbors.

Alexander Smith died on July 22, 1840. His wife, Sarah Jane (Leeper) Smith, survived him, dying on November 19, 1866. He made his Will on October 29, 1838, and it was proved, in Williamson County Court, on April 10, 1841. This document follows.

"In the name of God, Amen, I, Alexander Smith of Williamson County Tennessee, do make, ordain and constitute this my last will and testament, and, First, my primary object is to provide to the utmost extent of my power for my dear wife, in whom I have the most implicit confidence and to whose discretion I trust the disposition of all the property which may be given her by this will, believing that she will amply provide out of the same for our three children, James L. Smith, Benjamin D. Smith, and Susan D. Petway, we having heretofore given about two hundred acres of land to our daughter Elizabeth C. Hadley, the wife of Denny P. Hadley, also a negro woman together with some other property; also about two hundred acres of land to our daughter Emiline and her husband, Richard Christmas, and the further quantity of twenty-one acres in the corn, and (*sic* in transcript of will: in?) stead of a negro woman and the like amount of other property equal to that given Elizabeth C., . . . Therefore, believing as before stated that my wife . . . will provide amply for our three children, first above named.......... I hereby . . . give to her . . . all my land . . . and all my slaves . . . and, in a word, all of my property,............ I herein appoint my two sons, James L. Smith and Benjamin D. Smith, Executors of this my last will and testament, . . . In witness whereof, I have hereunto set my hand and seal this 29th day of October 1838,

Alex Smith."

The children of Alexander and Sarah Jane (Leeper) Smith:*

    i Elizabeth Clemmons Smith; described subsequently.

    ii James Leeper Smith; born December 12, 1801; married, and made his home in Texas.

    iii John C. (probably Clemmons) Smith; born November 19, 1803; died February 6, 1828.

---

*Recorded in a Bible, purchased by Alexander Smith, for nine dollars, in 1807.

- iv Stephen H. Smith; born December 12, 1805; died December 29, 1806.
- v Benjamin Drake Smith; described subsequently.
- vi Susannah Drake Smith; described subsequently.
- vii Mary Emeline Smith; described subsequently.

Elizabeth Clemmons Smith, the eldest child of Alexander and Sarah Jane (Leeper) Smith, received her middle name in memory of her paternal grandmother, Sarah Y. (Clemmons) Smith, mother of Alexander Smith. She was born January 23, 1800. She died in 1876. In 1821, she married Captain Denny Porterfield Hadley. He was a son of Captain Joshua Hadley, a soldier of the War of the Revolution. Captain Denny Porterfield Hadley was born in 1797, and died in 1871.

The children of Captain Denny Porterfield and Elizabeth Clemmons (Smith) Hadley were the following:

- i Amelia Hadley; born November 8, 1821; died August 27, 1822.
- ii William Hadley; born January 13, 1823.
- iii Sarah Jane Hadley; born February 29, 1824; died in 1898.
- iv Denny Porterfield Hadley, Junior; born May 11, 1825; married Susan Moore, in 1853.
- v John Smith Hadley; born in 1828; died in 1865.
- vi Mary Emeline Hadley; described subsequently.

Mary Emeline Hadley, just mentioned, was the youngest child of Captain Denny Porterfield and Elizabeth Clemmons (Smith) Hadley. She was born in 1835, and died in 1920. In 1856, she married Thomas Jones Clack. He was the grandson of Major John Clack, a member of the Legislature of Tennessee, continuously from 1796 to 1835. Major Clack's son, Spencer Clack, also, for many years, was a member of the Legislature. Whether the latter was the father of Thomas Jones Clack (husband of Mary Emeline Hadley), is not known to the compiler. Another son of Major John Clack was Judge Thomas M. Jones, of Pulaski, Tennessee. A brother of Thomas Jones Clack, above-mentioned, was Colonel Calvin Jones Clack.

Elizabeth Hadley Clack, daughter of Thomas Jones and Mary Emeline (Hadley) Clack, was born May 5, 1857. On August 20, 1873, she married William Blair Armistead. He was born June 14,

1848, and died June 4, 1935. He was the son of William Blair Armistead, Senior, whose wife was Mary Robina Woods. The last was a daughter of Robert Woods and his wife, Sarah (West) Woods, she being a daughter of Edward West, a silver-smith, of Lexington, Kentucky. A son of the last was William West, a celebrated artist, most of whose paintings were made in Europe (three of these being portraits of Lord Byron, who was his friend), and some of whose work is now in the Carnegie Library at Nashville, Tennessee, where he died in 1857.

The tradition has come down that, when Sarah West married Robert Woods, as mentioned above, she rode all the way to Philadelphia on horseback, to buy furniture, brocaded satin draperies, etc., for her new home.

Her husband, Robert Woods, was Nashville's first banker, and the site of his bank there was the southwest corner of the present Union Street and Third Avenue.

As already noted, Mary Robina Woods, daughter of Robert and Sarah (West) Woods, became the wife of William Blair Armistead, Senior, whose son, William Blair Armistead, Junior, married Elizabeth Hadley Clack. The elder Mr. Armistead was born in Charlottesville, Albemarle County, Virginia, close to the home of Thomas Jefferson. The Armistead family is a distinguished one. Anthony Armistead lived at Kirk Deighton, in Yorkshire, England. In 1608, he married Frances Thompson. Their son, William Armistead, came to Virginia about 1635, and died before 1660. The Coat-Armor borne by this family is blazoned as follows:

Arms—Or, a chevron between three spear-points sable tasseled in the middle.

Crest—A dexter arm in armor embowed proper, holding the butt-end of a broken spear.

Motto—Suivez raison—"Follow right."

The children of the aforesaid William Blair and Elizabeth Hadley (Clack) Armistead were:

    i Mary Robina Armistead; described below.

    ii William Woods Armistead; described below.

Mary Robina Armistead was born May 31, 1874. On January 25, 1891, she married James Washington Moore. He is the son of John Lawrence and Sarah Frances (Irby) Moore, and was born March 16, 1866, in Shelby County, Tennessee. His father, the said John Lawrence Moore, was born in Anson County, North Carolina, February 13, 1835, the son of Maurice Moore. James Washington Moore's mother, the said Sarah Frances (Irby) Moore, was born, April 2, 1841, in Madison County, Alabama, the daughter of Harrison Irby. She married John Lawrence Moore in Shelby County, Tennessee, January 30, 1862.

James Washington Moore, husband of Mary Robina Armistead, was educated entirely in Tennessee: at the private school of Captain Strickland, at Collierville; at Leddins Business College, at Memphis; and at Vanderbilt University, Nashville. He entered the University, 1886, received the degree of Bachelor of Arts, 1890, that of Bachelor of Laws, 1891, and was admitted to the Nashville Bar, September, 1891. He has been ever since a distinguished member of the legal profession, in Nashville, and in his State. 1903-1905, Mr. Moore represented Davidson County in the Tennessee House of Representatives. He was Assistant Attorney General of the Tenth Circuit, 1907-1908, and from September, 1910, to February, 1918, when he was appointed Assistant City Attorney of Nashville, holding this post till 1923, when he became City Attorney. He has remained in this office by re-appointment. Mr. Moore belongs to many professional, fraternal, and other organizations, and is a member of the Methodist Episcopal Church, South.

The children of James Washington and Mary Robina (Armistead) Moore are:

   i   James Washington Moore, Junior; born April 29, 1895.

   ii William Armistead Moore; born April 7, 1901.

   iii Mary Hadley Moore; born January 20, 1903; graduated, as Bachelor of Science, from George Peabody College for Teachers; later, attended Vanderbilt University; married, June 4, 1932, Donald Hardin Ragland, son of Mr. and Mrs. John Ragland, of Cookeville, Tennessee.

   iv Sarah Frances Moore; born March 24, 1907; December 1, 1928, married Edgar E. Rand, son of Mr. and Mrs. Frank Rand, of Saint Louis, Missouri; has children: Jeannette Hale Rand, born September 2, 1929; Mary Frances Rand, born December 3, 1930; Helen Octavia Rand, born September 14, 1932.

William Woods Armistead, son of the above-described William Blair and Elizabeth Hadley (Clack) Armistead, was born February 27, 1885. On June 12, 1918, he married Clara May Kelly. She is the daughter of Edward M. and Clara (Shivers) Kelly. Mr. Kelly occupied a high place in the milling and grain industry, being twice chosen President of the Millers' National Federation. He was also head of the Liberty Mills, long a President of the Southeastern Millers' Association, and was a prominent figure in the National Food Administration, during the World War. Mrs. Kelly died November 15, 1934, aged eighty-one. Mr. Kelly, son of Patrick B. Kelly of Ireland, died November 3, 1937.

The children of William Woods and Clara May (Kelly) Armistead are:

    i Clara Elizabeth Armistead; born May 1, 1919.

    ii Edmond Kelly Armistead; born January 25, 1923.

The known descendants of Elizabeth Clemmons Smith, the eldest child of Alexander and Sarah Jane (Leeper) Smith, have now been recorded herein. The next child, of whom descendants are known, was their fifth, Benjamin Drake Smith, listed above.

Benjamin Drake Smith was born March 8, 1808. He was a man of many talents, practised as a lawyer, became a Presbyterian Minister, and was highly esteemed in his community. It is said that he was a very handsome man. He resided near Brentwood, Tennessee, on part of the land granted to the heirs of his grandfather, Captain James Leeper. In the latter part of his life, he became blind, but, with true Christian courage and devotion, his daily prayer was the following: "Let us lay aside every weight and the sins which do so easily beset us, and run with patience the race of life set before us!"

Benjamin Drake Smith died on March 15, 1894. He was buried at Brentwood, beside his father and mother. There, too, was laid to rest, his wife. She was his cousin, Harriet Criddle, and they were married on May 3, 1832. An account of the Criddle family will appear later in this history.

The children of Benjamin Drake and Harriet (Criddle) Smith were the following:

    i John Criddle Smith; born December 1, 1834; married Mary Bradley, of Franklin, Tennessee; had no children.

    ii Mary Emeline Smith; born March 16, 1837; died in infancy.

    iii Amanda Elizabeth Smith; born November 2, 1839; died unmarried.

iv Laura Henrietta Smith; born April 25, 1843; married, first, ——— Mayfield; married, second ——— Pugh; had issue:

By first marriage:

1 Willie Mayfield; married Oscar Samuel Shannon, January 20, 1885; had a son, James Shannon, born October 14, 1886, who married, first, Cassie Conn, and had issue, James Henry, Martha, and Cassie Conn Shannon, and who, married, second, Bobbie Harmon; the said Oscar Samuel and Willie (Mayfield) Shannon having also a daughter, Lucile Shannon, who married Walter Wesley Alderman, June 9, 1913, and had children, as follows: William Hyram Alderman, born July 24, 1916; Lucile Shannon Alderman, born August 27, 1918; and Dorothy Jane Alderman, born September 11, 1919; another daughter of the said Oscar Samuel and Willie (Mayfield) Shannon being Bessie Shannon, who married, first, June 17, 1914, Fleming Cayce Burns, and had a son, Fleming Cayce Burns, Junior; married, second, October 8, 1919, her late husband's brother, James Rankins Burns, they now residing in Birmingham, Alabama, and having children: Thomas Shannon Burns, born July 18, 1920; William Edward Burns, born November 1, 1922.

By second marriage:

2 Florence Pugh; born June 8, 1872; married William Porter Howard, March 28, 1891; had children: Frank Howard, who died unmarried; and Laura Ellen Howard, born March 28, 1895, who married De Witt Ramsey of Statesville, North Carolina, and had two sons and one daughter.

v Susannah Savannah Smith; described below.
vi Alexander Livingston Smith; born January 17, 1850; died unmarried.

Sue Smith Gambill — *Wife of William Gambill*

William Gambill — *Husband of Sue Smith Gambill*

vii Sarah Elizabeth Smith; born December 26, 1852; married A. W. Downer; had a son, Albert Downer, whose wife's Baptismal name was Sylvia.

viii Benjamin Drake Smith, Junior; born June 22, 1856; died December 19, 1915; married Rowena Warren, who died about a year after their marriage, her husband never re-marrying.

Susannah Savannah Smith, the daughter of Benjamin Drake and Harriet (Criddle) Smith, was born November 27, 1846. She died in 1877. On January 17, 1872, by Reverend J. W. McDonald, she was married to William Frederick Gambill. Subsequently herein, will be described the ancestry of her husband, and record of their descendants will be given.

As already noted, Alexander Smith and his wife, Sarah Jane Leeper, the daughter of Captain James and Susan (Drake) Leeper, had, besides the children who, and whose descendants, have already been recorded in the present history, two other daughters: Susannah Drake Smith and Mary Emeline Smith. Some account will now be given of the elder of these.

Susan Drake Smith was born in 1811, and died in 1882. On February 2, 1832, she married Thomas Maury Petway. He was the son of Hinchey Petway and Susannah Caroline Parrish. They were married October 23, 1807. Hinchey Petway was the son of John Petway. The said Susannah Caroline Parrish was born May 25, 1789, in Lunenburg County, Virginia. From the records of Mrs. Walter Woolwine (born Susan Galbreath), has been gathered the following account of Susannah Caroline (Parrish) Petway's lineage. Mrs. Woolwine is her granddaughter.

Reverend James Fontaine, a Huguenot refugee, went from France to England in 1685. Other members of the Fontaine family accompanied him, as did also his betrothed, Anne Elizabeth Boursignote.* They were married on February 8, 1686. Their daughter, Mary Anne Fontaine, married in 1716, Matthew Maury. In 1719, they came to Virginia, and were great-grandparents of the famous Naval scientist, Matthew Fontaine Maury.

A son of the said Matthew and Mary Anne (Fontaine) Maury was Abraham Maury. He was born in Lunenburg County, Virginia, March 18, 1731, and died there, January 22, 1784. On September 2, 1759, he married Susannah Poindexter. She was born in Fluvanna

---

*This surname is usually given as Boursiquot.

SUSAN DRAKE SMITH AND HER HUSBAND, THOMAS MAURY PETWAY
(*Daughter of Alexander and Sarah Leeper Smith*)

County, Virginia, in 1746, and died in Williamson County, Tennessee, January 22, 1801.

Susannah Maury was the daughter of the said Abraham and Susannah (Poindexter) Maury. She was born June 24, 1764. In

1781, she married Joel Parrish, and they removed to Williamson County, Tennessee, near Franklin.

Susannah Caroline Parrish, daughter of Joel and Susannah (Maury) Parrish, as already stated, married Hinchey Petway, and they were the parents of the aforesaid Thomas Maury Petway, husband of Susan Drake Smith.

Mary Elizabeth Petway, daughter of Thomas Maury and Susan Drake (Smith) Petway, was born June 8, 1837. In the early 1850's, she married William Baine Galbreath, and their residence became Memphis, Tennessee. Mrs. Galbreath died in December, 1904. Her husband was born in 1828, near Hopkinsville, Kentucky. He was the youngest son of William Galbreath, born in Scotland, 1780, who came to America. He landed at Charleston, South Carolina, but soon removed to Wilmington, North Carolina, where he married Nancy McKinnon, in 1804. The following year, William and Nancy (McKinnon) Galbreath removed to Big West Fork, Christian County, Kentucky.

The children of the said William Baine and Mary Elizabeth (Petway) Galbreath were:

  i Thomas Maury Galbreath; born in Nashville, Tennessee, April 3, 1858; resides on Long Island, New York; married, April 27, 1892, in Memphis, Tennessee, Eugenia T. Edrington, born in Oceola, Arkansas, May 11, 1866, the daughter of James H. Edrington (born in Kentucky, October 2, 1829), and his wife, Nancy Bowen (born in Indiana, September 10, 1832); has a son, Thomas Maury Galbreath, Junior, born August 31, 1893, who married, June 15, 1918, Margaret Cameron (born in West Islip, Long Island, New York, November 16, 1894), and has children: Jean Cameron Galbreath, born in New York City, April 27, 1924; Duncan Cameron Galbreath, born in Islip, Long Island, New York, June 1, 1929.

  ii William Duncan Galbreath; died unmarried.

  iii Susan Ezelina Galbreath; married Walter Chapman Woolwine, May 17, 1888; had a daughter, Virginia Galbreath Woolwine, born August 21, 1892, who married, December 2, 1913, Alexander McDowell Smith of Lexington, Virginia, and had children: Susanne Galbreath Drake Smith, born January 10, 1915; Alexander McDowell Smith, Junior, born October 30, 1918.

iv Percy Baine Galbreath; resides in Memphis, Tennessee; married Kate Litton Chadwell, daughter of John Chadwell of Nashville, Tennessee; had children: William Duncan Galbreath, born August 15, 1907; Ann Litton Galbreath, Percy Galbreath died 1937; born April 5, and twins, Kate Litton Chadwell Galbreath and Sue

Mary Elizabeth Petway Galbreath *and daughter*,
Susan Ezelina Galbreath
(now Mrs. Walter Chapman Woolwine)

Chadwell Galbreath (who died in childhood), born January 28, 1915.

The youngest child, already mentioned herein, of Alexander and Sarah Jane (Leeper) Smith was Mary Emeline Smith. She was born in 1815, and died at the early age of twenty-seven years. She was buried in the old Smith resting-place, near Brentwood, Tennessee. Her husband was Colonel Richard Christmas, a large landowner in Tennessee and also in Mississippi, near Natchez, where, it is said, he owned so many slaves that he had a complete town laid off for them, each house with a garden-plot behind it.

Colonel Richard and Mary Emeline (Smith) Christmas had a son, Richard Christmas, Junior. While traveling in the West, he was murdered by a robber.

Account has now been given of the children of Alexander and Sarah Jane (Leeper) Smith,—the grandchildren of Captain James Leeper and Susan Drake, his wife,—together with account of their descendants, except in the case of the descendants of Susannah Savannah Smith, mentioned above. She, as already set forth herein, was the daughter of Benjamin Drake and Harriet (Criddle) Smith, Benjamin Drake Smith being son of Alexander and Sarah Jane (Leeper) Smith. Her birth, November 27, 1846, her death, in 1877, and her marriage, January 17, 1872, to William Frederick Gambill, have also been mentioned. Before showing the records of the descendants of William Frederick and Susannah Savannah (Smith) Gambill, the following history of the latter's Criddle family will be given, her mother being Harriet Criddle.

Criddle Family

FROM A NUMBER OF RECORDS, contributed by several descendants, the following account of this family has been made. Especially important as a source of information was Mrs. John Scruggs, who was born Mary Eliza Criddle, and who lived to the great age of ninety-four years, born in 1833 and died in 1927. She will be described subsequently. Another very valuable source was the Bible record of Alexander Smith, the husband of Sarah Jane Leeper, both of whom have already been described herein. His sister, Elizabeth Smith, married John Criddle.

The first ancestor traced was Allen Criddle, of Cumberland County, Virginia. His Will was made on May 5, 1777, and proved in 1778, the month and day unknown to the present compiler. Allen Criddle's wife was Ann, but her maiden surname has not been found. In the first census of the State of Virginia, considered as of the year 1790 (when the first census of the United States was prepared), but actually a very incomplete list of heads of families in Virginia, for the years 1782-1786, Ann Criddle appears as a household-head in Cumberland County, 1784. Her Will was made there, January 13, 1798, but the date of its proving is not among the records used for the present chronicle.

The children of Allen and Ann (———) Criddle were:

    i Susannah Criddle; described subsequently.
    ii Allen Criddle, Junior; appointed Executor of his mother's Will, 1798.
    iii John Criddle; described subsequently.
    iv Frances Criddle; married ——— Sanderson.
    v Ann Criddle; married ——— Richardson.
    vi Mary Criddle; married ——— Moss; had a son, Monroe Moss, who was a legatee in the Will of his aunt, Susannah Criddle, and also mentioned in the Will of the latter's son, John, both of which facts will again be stated herein.
    vii Finch Criddle.
    viii Elizabeth Criddle.

In the present study, lines of descent have been traced from two of the children of the foregoing Allen and Ann Criddle: their son, John; and their daughter, Susanna. Both of these branches are among the "Leeper-Drake Kith and Kin," and each will be described separately herein, as follows.

DESCENDANTS OF JOHN CRIDDLE, SON OF ALLEN AND ANN CRIDDLE

John Criddle was named in the Wills of his father, Allen Criddle, and his mother, Ann Criddle, both made in Cumberland County, Virginia. He was listed as head of a family in that County, in the census of 1782. The census-taker spelled his name "Creedle," and recorded that his family consisted then of five persons. These were, doubtless, himself, his wife, and his three eldest children, living in that year, and who will be named subsequently. As this is the only John Criddle of whom any mention has been found in Cumberland County at this period, it seems clearly evident that he was identical with John Criddle of Cumberland County who married Elizabeth Smith. He had a cousin of the same name, but the latter has been proven the son of Susannah Criddle (sister of John of Cumberland, thus, as already stated, daughter of Allen and Ann, and who, as will be shown, married a Criddle).

Elizabeth Smith, as sister of Alexander, which relationship was stated by Mrs. Scruggs, aforementioned as one of the chief authorities for the present Criddle history, was daughter of Robert and Sarah Y. (Clemmons) Smith. In the narrative which has already been set forth herein concerning the Smith family, the earliest record of this Robert Smith was a grant to him of land in North Carolina. It seems very probable that he was, earlier, a resident of Cumberland County, Virginia. In the Virginia census, 1782, were listed two men of this name, in Cumberland County. One Robert Smith had then five persons in his family, and the other Robert Smith had then a household of nine persons, also noted as having seven slaves. In this same census, the surname Clements (the original form of Clemmons, the family name of Robert Smith's wife), also is found.

Elizabeth (Smith) Criddle's brother, the said Alexander Smith, was the husband of Sarah Jane Leeper (daughter of Captain James Leeper and his wife, Susan Drake), and their descendants have already been described herein to considerable extent, while others will appear later.

Alexander Smith was born in 1769, and his sister, Elizabeth, who married John Criddle, must have been considerably his senior. In his Family Bible are written a number of Criddle items. The first of these, as to date, is of the birth, March 2, 1776, of Nancy

Criddle, daughter of John and Elizabeth Criddle. Assuming that Elizabeth was then at least eighteen years old, she would have been born in 1758, and, thus, would have been eleven years older than her brother, Alexander.

This same Bible record also mentions the following births of Criddle children, who were undoubtedly the children of John and Elizabeth (Smith) Criddle: John, August 27, 1780; Jesse, December 17, 1782; Frances, December 25, 1787 (her death noted as on September 29, 1806); Smith, February 21, 1790; Elizabeth, January 1, 1793. There is also record in Alexander Smith's Bible of the birth of Edward Criddle, son of *James* and Elizabeth Criddle, April 16, 1785; and other items not wholly legible. The name, James, however, seems very likely to have been an error made in transcription for John, the child, Edward, in that case, being among the children of John and Elizabeth (Smith) Criddle. This is doubtless correct, for nothing is known of a James Criddle at this time with a wife, Elizabeth. Therefore, this child, Edward, will be placed herein, presently, among the children of John and Elizabeth (Smith) Criddle. These children were:

    i   Ann ("Nancy") Criddle; described subsequently.

    ii Sarah Criddle, whose birth-date is not known, but who, it is probable, was born between Ann and the next child, John, since so long a period intervened,—four years; married John Jefferson, who was son of Field Jefferson, and, thus, brother to Peter Jefferson, this Peter being father of the great Thomas Jefferson, chief author of the immortal Declaration of Independence and President of the United States.

    iii John Criddle, Junior; described subsequently.

    iv Jesse Criddle; born December 17, 1782; perhaps died young, as no further record has been found concerning him.

    v   Edward Criddle; born April 16, 1785, whose mention in Alexander Smith's Bible record has been considered above; perhaps the Edward Criddle who built a stone house, 1806, in Jackson, Missouri.

    vi Frances Criddle; born December 25, 1787; died September 29, 1806.

    vii Smith Criddle; born February 21, 1790.

viii Elizabeth Criddle; born January 1, 1793.

Ann Criddle, called Nancy, in Alexander Smith's Bible, was born March 2, 1776. She married Thomas Battersby Balleu, whose lineage was as follows.

William Balleu, a French Huguenot, emigrated to Virginia. He married Dorothy Parker. They had a son, Thomas Balleu, who married Jane Thomas, said to have been daughter of the Lord Mayor of London. Thomas Balleu, Junior, son of Thomas and Jane (Thomas) Balleu, married Chloe Battersby, daughter of Lord William Battersby, Captain in the King's Life-Guards, before his settlement in Virginia, about 1775.

Thomas Battersby Balleu, husband of Ann Criddle, was son of the foregoing Thomas and Chloe (Battersby) Balleu. He and his wife had children:

    i Betsy Balleu; married O. D. Oliver; had a son, Olyntheus D. Oliver, who was born January 17, 1838, died February 10, 1901, who married Fannie Spain, December 15, 1864, and had daughters, Mattie (who married A. J. Haun), and Katie (who married C. L. Rhea); the aforesaid O. D. and Betsy (Balleu) Oliver having also three daughters, Betsy, Nancy, and Chloe.

    ii Thomas Battersby Balleu, Junior; married, and had sons, Thomas Battersby Balleu (the third of this name), and Robert Balleu.

    iii Leonard Criddle Balleu; married Helen McCowan, and had, with other children, a daughter, Eugenia Belleu, who married Rufus Gambill.

    iv Micah Balleu; married Jesse Thomas; had a daughter, Jane Thomas, born in Cumberland County, Virginia, September 2, 1800, who was author of "Early Days in Nashville."

    v Robert Smith Balleu; resided in Williamson County, Tennessee; married Martha Temple; and had children.

John Criddle, Junior, son of the above-described John and Elizabeth (Smith) Criddle, was born August 27, 1780. He died, aged forty-one, in 1821.

John Criddle married twice, his wives being sisters, and daughters of Jonathan and Lucy Drake. According to Mrs. John Scruggs, who was born Mary Eliza Criddle, and was mentioned at the beginning of this Criddle history, as a valued source of information, this Jonathan Drake was son of Benjamin Drake, who, in turn, was son of John and Margaret (Weldon) Drake. This last-mentioned couple were grandparents of Susan Drake, the wife of Captain James Leeper, and an extended account of this Drake family has already been given herein. It has been seen, in the said Drake history of the present work, that Benjamin Drake (son of John and Margaret and father of Susan Drake who married Captain Leeper), did have a son, Jonathan; and, from Mrs. Scruggs' record, have been learned the name of his wife, Lucy, as above-said, and the names of his two daughters, both of whom married John Criddle, Junior, together with the name of a third daughter of Jonathan and Lucy Drake, called Lucy, for her mother. This Lucy Drake became the grandmother of Hamilton Parks. Mrs. Scruggs narrates that Mr. Parks stated that his great-grandfather, Jonathan Drake, was born in 1754, that he was a poet, and that, because of the scarcity of printed books in his environment, he made copies of entire volumes.

The first wife of John Criddle, Junior, was Hannah Drake (daughter of Jonathan and Lucy, granddaughter of Benjamin and Mary,—"the Widow Smith,"—and great-granddaughter of John Drake and Margaret Weldon, his wife). Their marriage took place September 4, 1806.

The date of death of Hannah (Drake) Criddle is unknown, but the second marriage of her husband, John Criddle, Junior, took place, December 28, 1819. The second wife was Sarah Drake, sister of Hannah (Drake) Criddle. Sarah (Drake) Criddle died before July 31, 1834, when B. C. Drake was made Administrator of her Estate, as he stated in an Inventory of this, which was recorded August 25, 1834, in the Court of Davidson County, Tennessee.

Only two children are known to have been born to John Criddle, Junior, one by each marriage. These were:

    i Smith Criddle; described presently.

    ii Ewing Criddle; son of John and Sarah (Drake) Criddle; thirteen years old when his mother died, in or before 1834, and probably born in the year 1920 or the following year, his parents having been married in December, 1819; married Mary Ann ———, in 1843; probably died in 1845, as is indicated by a record of Mrs. Scruggs, which is not completely clear.

Smith Criddle, the elder son of John Criddle, Junior, and the latter's first wife, Hannah Drake, was born in 1808, as he was said by his daughter, Mrs. Scruggs, to have been aged thirty-seven years when he died, on November 20, 1845. On September 6, 1832, in Williamson County, Tennessee, he married Lucy Whitfield. That same autumn he and his wife removed from that County to Henry County, where they acquired a farm, seven miles from the town of Paris. After his death, his family returned to Williamson County. His wife died December 23, 1892.

The children of Smith and Lucy (Whitfield) Criddle were:

  i Mary Eliza Criddle; born in 1833, as she stated she was twelve years old when her father died in 1845; died at the end of December, 1927, as her funeral service was held on January 1, 1928; married, May 7, 1851 (her sixtieth anniversary being on May 7, 1911), John Scruggs, whose lineage is described subsequently, under Scruggs Family.

  ii Anna Criddle; married Doctor H. G. W. Grant.

  iii John H. Criddle; married and had a daughter, Anna Criddle, who married Alonzo Carroll, she dying in 1878, and her husband, for second wife, marrying ——— Howe, sister of Harry Howe of Nashville, Tennessee; said John H. Criddle also having daughters, Mary, who married Charles Bailey, and Maud, who died at the age of sixteen, and a son, Eugene Criddle, who became Mayor of Riverside, California.

  iv W. (probably, Whitfield, this being his mother's maiden surname) Smith Criddle; married Lenora Badger, whose second husband was Doctor W. H. Shuerman, born November 8, 1859, at Cincinnati, Ohio (son of C. Frederick and Henrietta Shuerman), for thirty-seven years Dean of Engineering, Vanderbilt University, and who died August 11, 1932; said W. Smith and Lenora (Badger) Criddle having sons: Charles Barrington, Whitfield, Edward, Smith, and Ewing Criddle.

There now has been set forth the record of known descendants of the first of the two Criddle lineages which, as already mentioned, belong among the "Leeper-Drake Kith and Kin," this said first Criddle lineage being that headed by John Criddle, Senior, son of Allen and Ann Criddle of Cumberland County, Virginia. Before proceeding to consideration of the second Criddle lineage, some account will be given of the Scruggs family, to which belonged John Scruggs, husband of Mary Eliza Criddle (daughter of Smith Criddle, granddaughter of John Criddle, Junior, great-granddaughter of John Criddle, Senior, and his wife, Elizabeth Smith, and great-great-granddaughter of Allen and Ann Criddle). The biography of the said Mary Eliza (Criddle) Scruggs has already appeared in its proper place in this first Criddle lineage.

Scruggs Family

RICHARD SCRUGGS, "Gentleman," came from Bedfordshire, in England, to Virginia, in 1655. Large Grants were made to him, comprising thousands of acres, in the Counties of James City and New Kent, some of these Patents bestowed upon him in consideration of his bringing Colonists to Virginia.

Henry Scruggs, son of Richard Scruggs, the Colonist, lived in New Kent County, Virginia. On January 25, 1685, in Saint Peter's Parish, he married Anne Grose.

Richard Scruggs, son of Henry and Anne (Grose) Scruggs, was granted two hundred and fifty acres of land in Goochland County, Virginia. His wife's Baptismal name was Martha.

Drury Scruggs was the son of Richard and Martha Scruggs He was born in New Kent County, February 1, 1725. Later, he re moved to Cumberland County, Virginia, where he died, after Apri 29, 1782, the date of his Will. His wife was Mary Carter.

Edward Scruggs, son of Drury and Mary (Carter) Scruggs, settled in Botetourt County, Virginia, and was a wealthy planter there. His son, Edward Scruggs, Junior, went, with two brothers, into Tennessee, where his home was in Williamson County. He is described as "a genial, quiet man, greatly beloved." He died on his estate in 1846. Edward Scruggs, Junior, married, in 1818, Apha Hassell. She was the daughter of Joseph Hassell, who fought in the War of 1812, under General Andrew Jackson.

The children of Edward and Apha (Hassell) Scruggs were Thomas, William, Joseph, Edward, John, Nancy, Frederick, Drury, and Young Scruggs. Of these, John Scruggs became the husband of Mary Eliza Criddle.

The said John Scruggs was born August 20, 1826. He, and his brothers, were educated at "Old Franklin Academy," at Franklin, Tennessee. He died at Nashville, Tennessee, March 28, 1911. His marriage to Mary Eliza Criddle, as has been mentioned above herein, took place on May 7, 1851. As also mentioned, his wife survived him, dying, at the great age of ninety-four, in December, 1927. Of her it has been said: "Mrs. Mary Scruggs was a lovely Christian character. Everyone loved her who knew her."

The only child of John and Mary Eliza (Criddle) Scruggs (or, certainly, the only child living on John Scruggs' death), was Edward Criddle Scruggs. He was born on the estate of his grandfather,

Edward Scruggs, in Williamson County, Tennessee. This was located five miles from Franklin, the County Seat. In 1901, Edward Criddle Scruggs married Elizabeth Stuart. She was the daughter of Colonel Samuel and Mary (Bothwell) Stuart, of Pittsburgh, Pennsylvania, and the granddaughter of William Stuart.

Edward Criddle Scruggs, Junior, is the son of Edward Criddle and Elizabeth (Stuart) Scruggs. He was born October 17, 1902. On June 12, 1924, he married Annie Lou Mimms. He and his wife have two sons: Edward Criddle Scruggs, Third, born April 4, 1926; and Maurice Henry Scruggs, born August 11, 1929.

The foregoing is the outline-chronicle of the Scruggs lineage, so far as it is connected with the present history. But more should be set forth concerning Edward Criddle Scruggs, the Elder, son of John and Mary Eliza (Criddle) Scruggs, for he was a most remarkable and admirable character.

In his boyhood, he was blinded, by the accidental discharge of a gun, during a hunting expedition. Nevertheless, he became an outstanding man in his community, highly respected, and a successful builder of houses. When his maternal uncle, W. Smith Criddle, died, he appointed Edward Criddle Scruggs his Executor, also making him Guardian of the Testator's five little sons. A few years ago, an account of Mr. Scruggs was published in the *American Magazine*. His mother, Mrs. Mary Eliza (Criddle) Scruggs, was then still living, and she narrated the following concerning her son.

"Mr. Dutton of Philadelphia (Staff Representative of the *American Magazine*) came to Nashville, and a prominent business-man gave him Ed's address. He came to see him, and asked how he ever came to build houses. Ed said:

" 'One day a group of neighbors assembled at his father's house, and, of course, the blind boy was the topic of conversation. One man said: "If he were my son, he should never do a stroke of work. He has suffered enough, without having to pay his own way in the world. I would do it for him, if I had to work my fingers to the bone." "Yes," agreed another, "the world owes him a living, and 'twould be a downright shame for him to have to work for one,—and what could he possibly do?" After they left, Doctor Cliff placed his hand on Ed's shoulder, and said: "Ed, they mean well, but don't listen to them. They all set to make a loafer of you, but don't you let them. There are things lots worse than being blind: one of them is being good-for-nothing.

" 'One man said: "Scruggs, I will give you my eyes for your brain." An attorney of much ability said: "Mr. Scruggs, I would get me a good street-corner, and sell pencils and shoe-strings." Ed said, laughingly: "My soul! To sell shoe-strings would be a task!" One day W. S. Criddle came in and said: "Ed, I have it! Why not build houses?" And that settled it.'

"A number of years ago, Doctor Wampler, of the Blind School, had made one thousand copies of the sketch of Ed's career, written by Miss Sinclair, relative to his industrious traits, which he distributed for the benefit of the blind throughout the Union."

Resuming the consideration of Criddle ancestry (in whose record belongs the account just given of the Scruggs family), and having now completed the first Criddle lineage,—that of descendants of John Criddle, Senior, son of Allen and Ann Criddle,—the following will now be described:

Descendants of Susannah Criddle, Daughter of Allen and Ann Criddle

Susannah Criddle evidently married a kinsman, for she was named as a daughter of Ann Criddle, in the latter's Will, January 13, 1798, and therein called "Susannah Criddle." Her husband's name is not known. The possibility that she was a daughter-in-law of Ann Criddle seems eliminated; for, in such case, she would doubtless have been explicitly described in the latter's Will, as the wife, or widow, of a son of the Testator.

There was a "Hannah Credle," listed as head of a household in Mecklenburg County, Virginia, in the census of 1782. "Hannah" and "Susannah" are often found used interchangeably in old records, and it may be that she was Susannah Criddle of present consideration, and then a widow.

Susannah Criddle later lived in Davidson County, Tennessee, probably going there in the company of her son, John Criddle, to be described subsequently. She died there, between March 3, 1823, when her Will was dated, and October 30, 1829. The latter date was that of her said son's Will, in which he mentioned a certain legacy as having been made in his mother's Will. It is this mention, indeed, which has completely identified the said John Criddle as the son of Susannah Criddle. Her Will has been transcribed as follows:

"In the name of God, Amen. I Susannah Criddle of Davidson County, Tenn., being in a sound and unimpaired mind though of a weak and feeble body, do make and ordain this my last Will and Testament (to wit)

"In the first place I give and bequeath to my nephew Monroe Moss, one hundred dollars to be paid to him when he arrives at the age of twentyone years. My Executor, hereinafter mentioned. (Thus, in the transcription, perhaps correctly, "By my Executor," &c. *The Compiler*) Secondly I give and bequeath to my son John Criddle at my death all my other property of every description with this provision that he is to give to his children, when how and in the way I form ("and form"—?: *The Compiler*) that he may think best.

"Thirdly, I do hereby revoke all other Wills and Testaments which may heretofore have been made by me.

"Fourthly, I do constitute and appoint my son John Criddle my sole and only Executor to carry into effect this my last Will and Testament.

"Fifthly and lastly I do will that security shall not be required of my son John Criddle as my Executor to act hereupon in Testimony whereof I have hereunto set my hand and seal this third day of March Eighteen Hundred and Twenty Three."

In the transcription of this Will, the Testatrix' name,—though correctly given as "Susannah," in the beginning of the Will,—is written, "Savannah," as the signature. This is doubtless an error of the modern copyist. The Will is recorded on Page 366, Book 9, in the Court House, Nashville, Tennessee. It was witnessed by Smith Criddle and Robert Trotter. This witness, Smith Criddle, was probably Smith Criddle, son of John and Elizabeth (Smith) Criddle, born in 1790, as noted above herein. He is the only known man of this name, old enough to have witnessed a Will in 1823. The next Smith Criddle (son of John Criddle, Junior, by his first wife, Hannah Drake), was born in 1808, and would have been a minor in 1823, when Susannah Criddle's Will was witnessed. The Smith Criddle, born in 1790, and witness to this Will, was nephew to the Testatrix, as son of her brother, John Criddle, Senior (husband of Elizabeth Smith).

Mrs. Susannah Criddle had but one child, so far as any record shows. This was John Criddle, named Executor of her Will, as above stated. There has been some confusion in the knowledge of Criddle descendants as to the identity and relationships of the three early Johns of this surname. But study of the records places them as herein described: (1) John Criddle, son of Allen and Ann

Criddle, and named in their Wills; (2) John Criddle, Junior, son of John and Elizabeth (Smith) Criddle, the last John, without doubt, John, the son of Allen and Ann Criddle; (3) John Criddle, son of Susannah Criddle, and who is now to be described.

John Criddle, son of ———— and Susannah (Criddle) Criddle, was, far as has been discovered, the only child of his parents. As already stated, he was appointed Executor of his mother's Will, in 1823. It seems probable that her death had occurred not long before his own Will was made, and that her own Estate had not then been settled appears certain, for he wrote in this document the following: "it was willed by my mother that her nephew Monroe Moss should have one hundred dollars when he arrived at the age of twentyone years. I wish that legacy to be paid him." This said nephew of Mrs. Susannah Criddle (and, thus, first cousin of John, her son), was the child of Mary Criddle, daughter of Allen and Ann Criddle, whose husband was ———— Moss, as has already been mentioned above herein.

John Criddle died between October 30, 1829, the date of his Will, and the Session of the Court of Davidson County, Tennessee, January, 1830, when his Will was proved. It has been transcribed as follows:

"In the name of God Amen: I John Criddle of Davidson County and State of Tenn. being weak of body but of sound and unimpaired mind, do constitute and make this my last will and Testament in the form and words following: To wit, In the first place I will that my land on which I now live be sold on a credit of four eight twelve sixteen twenty and twentyfour months for the purpose of raising money to pay my part of a debt of two thousand four hundred dollars due the Branch Bank of the United States at Nashville by Robert Lanier and myself, my part of debt being one thousand three hundred dollars to secure the payment of which I have heretofore given a mortgage upon the land above mentioned and also upon two negroes Jack and Randal. The balance of the money arising from the sale of said land I wish to be applied to the payment of my other just debts. If that balance should be insufficient I wish the money arising from the sale of my stock of every description, my household and kitchen furniture and my crop to be applied to the payment of my debts so that none of my negroes may be sold.

"Secondly, I will that my negroes be hired out and enough of the money arriving from that hire be reserved to board, school and clothe decently my three youngest children, Harriet, Amanda and James until the girls marry or arrive at the age of eighteen years and until James shall have acquired a good English education and be bound to some trade I wish him to have the choosing of.

"Thirdly, I give to my daughter Harriet Criddle a negro girl named Prisilla and also a good feather bed and furniture.

"Fourthly, I give and bequeath to my daughter Amanda Criddle a negro girl named Nancy and also a good feather bed and furniture.

"Fifthly, I give and bequeath to my son James Criddle a negro boy named William.

"Simply it is my will that all the property of every kind which I may own after the provision for my three youngest children (which provision is mentioned in the second article of this will) be complied with and after the legacies mentioned above shall be taken out be equally divided amongst all my children and my two grandchildren John Lanier and Susan Lanier, giving to these John and Susan the part which their mother Eliza Lanier should have had, if she had lived, that is one fifth part between the two after taking out the worth of Sylva (a negro girl given by me to their mother Eliza) from the first one fifth part.

"Seventhly, I wish Robert Lanier father of my grandchildren John and Susan to have the power of selling the first negro girl Sylva and all other property which by this will may go to the first* children John and Susan or make any disposition of all or any part of 2nd (*sic: The Compiler*) property which to him may seem best for the interest of his children and 2nd, (?—perhaps, correctly, "the said": *The Compiler*) John and Susan Lanier.

"Eighthly, I wish the land, stock furniture herein before mentioned to be sold as soon as possible after my decease. The stock, furniture, etc., at twelve months credit.

"Ninthly, it was willed by my mother that her nephew Monroe Moss should have one hundred dollars when he arrived at the age of twentyone years. I wish that legacy to be paid him.

"Tenthly, I appoint my friend John Hobson my executor to carry into effect this my last will and Testament. This will was made sealed and signed with my own hand this 30th day of October 1829

"John Criddle"

---

*The word, "first," in this part of the Will appears in the latter's transcript, but may be an error in copying, for "said."

The foregoing Will was witnessed by Smith Criddle, William Weakley, and John Finks. As has been mentioned, above, in describing the Will of Susannah Criddle (mother of John, whose Will has just been set forth), this Smith Criddle was doubtless the Smith Criddle, born in 1790, son of John and Elizabeth (Smith) Criddle. He was, thus, nephew to Susannah Criddle, and first cousin to her son, John Criddle, of the foregoing Will.

John Criddle added a codicil to his Will, but the date is not clear in the transcript made. This codicil reads:

"I give and bequeath to my grandchild John C. Lanier, one hundred acres of land which I own in Summer County and which I bought of Robert Eaton and which lies on Drake's Creek. I give this in addition to the provision made for him in the above will."

A condensed account of D. B. Love, acting as Guardian to one of the three minor children of John Criddle, Harriet Criddle, presented to Davidson County Court, July Session, 1831, shows that the following property for her came to his charge, February 19, 1830: a negro girl, Priscilla, aged seven years, and a third of the total number of negroes who had belonged, it is evident, to the Estate of Harriet Criddle's father, her share in them being described as "Hannah and child Harriet, Lucy and child Minerva, Ginney and Milbry." In a return to the Court of expenses incurred for Harriet Criddle, her Guardian is given his full name, David B. Love. He had paid, on behalf of his Ward, among other items, a sum of twenty-three dollars and seventy-five cents to Alexander Smith, "for board and shoes," and ten dollars to James Ellis, "for tuition."

In a Petition, whose transcript is not dated, but which was recorded, in Davidson County, Court, December 7, 1832, Benjamin D. Smith and his wife, Harriet S. Smith (who was Harriet, daughter of the John Criddle of present consideration, and whose middle name may have been Susannah, for her paternal grandmother), evidently asked that a division be made of the negroes belonging to Harriet's late father. The Court appointed the following commissioners for this office: John Thompson, Hinchey Petway, Jack McGavock, Joseph L. Ewing, and Hugh W. McGavock. Apparently, the full list of negroes was "Lucy, Jenny, Hannah, Milly, Minerva, Harriet, and an unnamed "infant."

It seems indicated that John Criddle had been twice married, and that his second wife had died when he made his Will, since no reference appears therein to a wife. As he left three minor children, and had grandchildren, it may be supposed that he had children by both of his two marriages. As he divided a part of his property bequeathed in his Will in fifth parts, it is evident that he had five children. Of these, one, Eliza, had died, leaving two children, legatees in John Criddle's Will. He named therein his three youngest, and minor, children: Harriet, Amanda, and James. He did not name a daughter, Adaline Criddle, but she is known by descendants to have been daughter of a John Criddle, and to have been born in 1802. On that date, there was no John Criddle known, who could have been her father, except the foregoing John, son of Mrs. Susanna Criddle. The date of death of the John Criddle who married Elizabeth Smith is not known, but there seems no evidence that he married any other wife than Elizabeth, and none that he had a daughter, Adaline. His son, John Criddle, Junior, born in 1780, might, it is true, have married before his first known marriage, in 1806, to Hannah Drake, and, thus, have had a child born in 1802; but there seems no reason to suppose this. But it is evident that the John Criddle, son of Susanna, and who made his Will in 1829, as above described, did have another child, besides those named in his Will, who were: Eliza, then deceased, and the three youngest, Harriet, Amanda, and James. Therefore, Adaline Criddle, known to be daughter of a John Criddle, and born in 1802, seems undoubtedly to have been child of John Criddle son of Susannah. A statement has been made that her mother's maiden surname was McGavock, but this may have been a confusion of memory, since McGavock was apparently the middle name of her husband, and was the middle name of her son, as will be described subsequently.

Summarizing the preceding, it may be stated that John Criddle, son of Mrs. Susannah Criddle, probably was twice married, but that the names of his wives are not known. His children were:

    i Eliza Criddle; perhaps not the eldest child, but evidently one of the two eldest known children of John Criddle (son of Mrs. Susannah Criddle); married Robert Lanier; had a son, called grandchild in the Will of John Criddle, 1829-1830, John C. (probably Criddle) Lanier; also had a daughter, Susan Lanier, who married ——— Hull.

    ii Adaline Criddle; described subsequently.

    iii Harriet Criddle; described subsequently.

    iv Amanda Eleanor Criddle; described subsequently.

v James Criddle; a minor in 1829, when his father's Will was made.

Adaline Criddle, just listed among the children of John Criddle (son of Mrs. Susannah Criddle), was born June 14, 1802. She died January 8, 1870. On July 4, 1820, she became the wife of William M. Hinton. He was born December 7, 1799, and died August 27, 1854.

James McGavock Hinton, son of William M. and Adaline (Criddle) Hinton, was born January 22, 1827. He died March 7, 1897. His marriage to Olivia J. Andrews took place April 18, 1849. She was born in 1831, and died July 7, 1870. The children of James McGavock and Olivia J. (Andrews) Hinton were the following:

i Addie Hinton; married, September 15, 1886, Edward T. Lowe, founder of E. T. Lowe Publishing Company, one of the outstanding figures of the printing industry in the South, and who died at his home in Nashville, Tennessee, August 31, 1931; had children:

1 Addie Hinton Lowe; born November 11, 1887; married Norman W. Jeffries; had a daughter,

HARRIET CRIDDLE SMITH

BENJAMIN DRAKE SMITH

        born October 16, 1912, who was given the name of her father, Norman W. Jeffries.

   2 Edward T. Lowe, Junior; born June 29, 1890; married Helen Cady; had children: Betty Alden Lowe, born March 2, 1917; and Edith Hearst Lowe, born April 23, 1928; resides in Beverly Hills, Los Angeles County, California.

ii Olivia J. Hinton; married J. Q. Holt.
iii Selina J. Hinton.
iv William E. Hinton.
v James Criddle Hinton; died May 30, 1932.
vi Minnie Noel Hinton; twin to the preceding.
vii Lemira Bowling Hinton; married James W. Fall, May 10, 1894.

    Harriet Criddle, daughter of John Criddle, who was son of Mrs. Susannah Criddle, as above set forth, has already been mentioned herein under account of the Smith Family, as she married Benjamin Drake Smith, on May 3, 1832.

She was born August 20, 1814, and died February 18, 1898. Record of her children and descendants has already appeared in this history, with the exception of those of her daughter, Susannah Savannah Smith, who married, as stated above herein, William Frederick Gambill. Data on the Gambill family and on the descendants of William Frederick and Susannah Savannah (Smith) Gambill will be narrated subsequently.

The aforesaid Harriet Criddle has been called a cousin of her husband, Benjamin Drake Smith. Actual relationship, however, does not appear proven. There was a kinship, however, though not in blood, because of the two marriages of another John Criddle to daughters of Jonathan and Lucy Drake. This other John Criddle, already described herein, was John Criddle, Junior, son of John and Elizabeth (Smith) Criddle, the last mentioned John (husband of Elizabeth Smith) being, it seems impossible to doubt, son of Allen and Ann Criddle, the said Allen and Ann being parents also of Susannah Criddle, who married ——— Criddle, and (as has been told herein), was grandmother to Harriet Criddle, who married Benjamin Drake Smith aforesaid.

Amanda Eleanor Criddle, youngest daughter of the above-described John Criddle (son of Mrs. Susannah Criddle) remains now to be mentioned.

She was a minor in 1829, when her father made his will. She became the wife of Charles James Fox Wharton. He was son of George Wharton of Virginia, whose father, John Wharton, came to Virginia from England as a young boy. This family is called that of Lord Philip Wharton, probably the famous Duke of Wharton of that name.

The children of Charles James Fox and Amanda Eleanor (Criddle) Wharton were:

   i Samuel Wharton; married Mollie Montague Woolwine; had children:

      1 Emma Woolwine Wharton.

      2 Samuel Seay Wharton.

      3 Mary Wharton.

  ii Aurelia Wharton; died unmarried.

 iii John Criddle Wharton; died unmarried.

- iv G. Eugene Criddle Wharton; a soldier in the Civil War; killed, at the age of eighteen, October 8, 1862, in the Battle of Perryville, Kentucky.
- v Aaron White Wharton; married Tennie Halliburton, June 10, 1872.
- vi Charles James Fox Wharton, Junior; died unmarried.
- vii May Wharton; died unmarried.
- viii Alice Wharton; described presently.
- ix Octavia Wharton.

Alice Wharton, just mentioned, the eighth child of Charles James Fox and Amanda Eleanor (Criddle) Wharton, married Woolridge Bullock,—known as "Dick" Bullock. They resided in Franklin, Tennessee. Mr. Bullock was eminent as a lawyer, an editor, and a writer, under the *nom-de-plume* of "Harpeth." The following is related of him.

In the early part of the year 1880, Mr. Bullock was in the city of Washington. While there, he was a guest of Clark Mills, the sculptor, who showed him the statue he had made of Andrew Jackson. Mr. Bullock was so impressed with the work that he wrote to several Tennessee newspapers, suggesting that the statue be purchased for the State by popular subscription, and erected in the Capitol grounds at Nashville. The idea met with wide and prompt enthusiasm; the money for the purchase was raised in a few weeks; and, May 20, 1880, the statue was unveiled on its present site, in the grounds of Tennessee's Capitol. The sculptor, in token of appreciation, made a bust of Mr. Bullock, presenting it to the latter.

The children of Thomas Woolridge and Alice (Wharton) Bullock were:

- i Amanda Eleanor Wharton Bullock.
- ii Annie Mary Bullock; described presently.
- iii Elizabeth Bullock.

Annie Mary Bullock, just mentioned, daughter of Thomas Woolridge and Alice (Wharton) Bullock, married William Yandell Elliott. He was a graduate of the Law School of Vanderbilt University at Nashville, Tennessee.

The children of William Yandell and Annie Mary (Bullock) Elliott were:

- i William Yandell Elliott, Junior; described below.

ii Richard Wharton Elliott; received his preliminary education at the Webb Preparatory School; graduated from Vanderbilt University; resides on a fruit-ranch, at Mecca, California; married Edith Hammond; has children:
    1 Richard Wharton Elliott, Junior.
    2 Anne Mary Elliott.

William Yandell Elliott, Junior, mentioned above as elder son of William Yandell and Annie Mary (Bullock) Elliott, received his Degree as Bachelor of Arts from Vanderbilt University in 1917. In 1920, the same institution conferred upon him the Degree of Master of Arts. He received the great distinction of a Rhodes Scholarship, attending Balliol College at Oxford University in England, whence, in 1923, he received the Degree of Doctor of Philosophy.

A patriot as well as scholar, William Yandell Elliott, Junior, served in the World War. He was a member of Battery E, at Camp Sevier, in Tennessee, with rank of Second Lieutenant, and later First Lieutenant in Battery D. In 1918, he went overseas with the American Expeditionary Forces.

After the Armistice, while in Paris, he attended lectures at the Sorbonne. During his last year at Vanderbilt University, he had been Assistant in the Department of English. Later, he taught for two years in the Political Science Department of the University of California. Since 1925, he has been Professor of Government at Harvard University. In connection with research work for Harvard, Doctor Elliott was sent, by the Harvard and Radcliffe Board of International Research to England. In the same connection, he attended sessions of the League of Nations at Geneva. He has won distinction as a lecturer and as a writer on governmental and political themes.

William Yandell Elliott, Junior, married Barbara Foster, of Boston. Her father was Associate Editor of *The Youth's Companion*, and, later, of *The Philadelphia Inquirer*.

The children of William Yandell and Barbara (Foster) Elliott are:
    i William Yandell Elliott, III.
    ii Paul Pinkerton Foster Elliott.
    iii Charles James Fox Wharton Elliott.

Ewing Family

IN AN EARLIER PART of this history of Leeper-Drake Kith and Kin, under account of the family of Alexander Smith, husband of Sarah Jane Leeper, only child of Captain James Leeper and Susan Drake, his wife, mention has been made of the said Alexander Smith's sister, Sarah, whose descendants will now be described.

Sarah Smith, daughter of Robert and Sarah Y. (Clemmons) Smith, married Captain Alexander Ewing. She was born August 12, 1761, and is erroneously stated to have died June 15, 1810. The year, 1810, could not have been that of her death, for she was living, February 6, 1822, when her husband's Will was made, in which she is named. She was buried in the old Ewing graveyard, which has been described as "situated about one and a half miles from the old Love place on Ewing's Creek. Boyd's creek runs through the Love place and it and Ewing's creek are within sight of each other." Ewingville, a suburb of Franklin, Tennessee, and named for this family, occupies the land granted them by the State of North Carolina, in which the present Tennessee was then included. Probably, this grant was made because of the services of Captain Alexander Ewing, husband of Sarah Smith, who was a soldier of our War for Independence.

Captain Ewing died between February 6, 1822, the date when he signed his Will, and April of the same year, when the Will was presented at the Court of Davidson County, Tennessee. This document follows:

"I, Alexander Ewing of Davidson county, State of Tennessee, do make and publish my last will and testament as follows:

"I give and bequeath to my beloved wife, Sally, during her natural life, one third part of all my lands I possess in Davidson county including the Mansion house and houses and all other buildings on the tract of land I now reside (on?—*the transcriber*) to be laid off by my executors hereinafter named. Also, I give to her during her natural life the use of one half of the stock upon my farm and farming utensils to be divided by my said executors. Also the whole of the household and kitchen furniture with the exception of bed furniture which are to be divided by my said executors between her and my three sons, Alexander, Randall McGavock and William Black, taking unto such division the beds and bed furniture which have recently been given to Alexander and Randall or which may be given to them previous to my death. It being my desire that my wife should not be restricted in the disposition or sale of any of the above personal property bequested to her as aforesaid, but that she should sell or dispose of such part thereof as she may think necessary or proper. Also I give to her during her natural life one half of all the slaves of which I may be possessed except those hereinafter specifically bequeathed to be divided by my said executors.

"I give to my son James Ewing and his heirs forever a tract of land on Smith's fork of Caney Fork in Wilson county, containing six hundred and forty acres. Also the slaves now in his possession. To wit: George and Sarah, his wife, Lucy, Polly Peggy, Washington and Jack, together with their increase. Also twenty-five shares of the capital stock of the Bank of the State of Tennessee. Third, I give to my son, Alexander Ewing and his heirs, forever, one half of the tract of land in Williamson county near Franklin containing five hundred and thirty-eight acres. Also two lots or parts of lots in the town of Nashville on Water Street which were conveyed by Hall and McNairy to C. Stump by him to Thomas Shute and by him to me. Also the following slaves, Andrew, and his wife Milley, and her children, Cynthia excepted. Also, Tom, Phillis, Henry and Rhoda, also twenty-five shares of the Capital stock of the Bank of the State of Tennessee.

"Fourth, I give to my son Randall McGavock Ewing and his heirs forever, the other half of said tract of land of four hundred and thirty-eight acres (this tract, above in the Will, described as *five* hundred and thirty-eight acres: the compiler) to be equally divided as to quality and quantity between him and said Alexander by my said executors, should I not make a division thereof between them in my life time. Also a part of lot number six in the town of Nashville on Water Street including Stump's warehouse which was conveyed by James Trimple, also by Thomas Shute to me. Also the following slaves to wit: Caesar and China his wife and her children, also Phoebe, Ezekiel, Bob and Judy. Also fifty shares of the Bank stock of the Nashville Bank.

"Fifth, I give to my grandson, William Black Ewing and his Heirs, forever, the tract of land, whereon I now live in Davidson county, containing five hundred acres, subject to the life of my beloved wife, therein (*sic:* the compiler) before mentioned, also sixty acres of land on Stone's river in Rutherford county. Also the other half of the stock, farming utensils, also upon the death of my beloved wife, the stock farming utensils, household and kitchen furniture which may remain upon my farm, the use and disposition of which is bequeathed to her as aforesaid also the other half of my slaves which I may be dispossessed (*sic:* the compiler) as aforesaid with the exception of those specifically bequeathed and upon the death of my beloved wife the said slaves and their increase which are bequeathed to her during her life are to be equally divided by my said executors between my said sons, Alexander, Randall McGavock and William Black, also I give to my said son, William Black, fifty shares of the Capital stock of the Nashville Bank.

"Sixth, I give to my grandson Elexander Ewing McGavock and his heirs forever a tract of land containing three hundred twenty acres on LoosaHatchee river in the eleventh district in Range two section four.

"Seventh, I give to my grandson Oscar Smith Ewing and his heirs forever a tract of land containing three hundred acres in the eleventh district in range three section seven.

"Eighth, I give to my grand daughter Nancy Kent McGavock and her heirs my negro girl slave named Cynthia and her increase, provided my granddaughter should live to attain the age of eighteen years or should marry, but should neither of these events happen the said slave and her increase are to be divided with the residue of my estate hereinafter named mentioned. (*Sic:* the compiler).

"Ninth, I give to my son, William Black my gold watch.

"Tenth, All the rest and residue of my lands not hereinbefore specifically divided, I give to my sons, James Alexander, Randall McGavock and William Black and their heirs forever.

"Eleventh, All the rest and residue of my personal estate of every description not herein specifically bequeathed after the payment of my just debts, I give and bequeath to my beloved wife and my sons Alexander, Randall McGavock and William Black and their heirs forever.

"Twelfth, All the aforesaid devises and bequests to my son Alexander Ewing are to depend on the contingency that he does not marry Sarah Jefferson, and in the event that he should not comply with my desire in that particular and should marry her, he is to take nothing under the will, but all and enduring the devises and bequests to him aforesaid as there unto to vest in my sons Randall McGavock and William Black and their heirs and lastly I do hereby constitute and appoint my friend (friends? the compiler) Oliver B.

Hayes and William L. Brown and my son Alexander Ewing Jr. executors of this my last will and testament, hereby revoking all others by me heretofore made. In that part of my estate respecting which my son Alexander is to (be? the compiler) legatee or devised he is not to act and I do hereby direct that my aforesaid executors shall not be required to give bond and security previous to their taking letters testamentary and etc. Witness my hand and seal this February 6, 1822.

"Alexander Ewing.

"Signed, sealed and declared in presence of us the word 'personal' in the first item being first interlined and the erasure there in first made.

"Jac McGavock
Robert W. Green
Jacob Perkins.

"State of Tennessee, Davidson county court, April Session 1822. A paper writing purporting to be the last will and testament of Alexander Ewing deceased was produced in open court and proved thus Jacob McGavock and Robert W. Green two of the subscribing Witnesses being duly sworn say they became such in the presence of the testator and at his request, and that they believe he was in his right mind at the time of executing said paper writing. It is therefore ordered that the same be entered of record as such will of Alexander Ewing deceased and thereupon Oliver B. Hayes, William L. Brown, Alexander Ewing, Jr. the executors named in said will came into court and qualified as such, ordered that they have letters testamentary granted to them."

It is difficult to record, with positive assurance of accuracy, the children of Captain Alexander Ewing, maker of the foregoing Will. In that document, after its provision for his wife, he mentioned "my son James Ewing." In one instance, he mentioned "my sons, James Alexander, Randall McGavock and William Black." In other instances, he mentioned "my sons Alexander, Randall McGavock and William Black." He bequeathed to "my grandson, William Black Ewing," but, later in the same part of the Will, he said: "also I give to my said son, William Black. . . ." When the testator named grandchildren, he did not state their parents' names. Therefore, the following account is made of the children and descendants of Captain Alexander and Sarah (Smith) Ewing, as gathered from statements in his Will, together with facts known to the author from personal association. The exact order of births is not known; though the sons were probably born in the order given, since, in their father's Will, they were thus named.

    i James Ewing; legatee in the Will of Captain Alexander Ewing; as said above, named first in that Will, after the testator's wife; attention being called, however, to the possibility, noted above, that James was the first name of the following Alexander Ewing, Junior

   ii Alexander Ewing, Junior; legatee in his father's Will. and an Executor of that Will; forbidden therein, under penalty of disinheritance, to marry Sarah Jefferson; evidently died unmarried, from his Will, the date of which is not given in the copy furnished the compiler, but which copy is headed, "A. Ewing Deceased, Will, October 1850," which Will follows.

"In the name of Almighty God, Amen, I, Alexander Ewing, of the county of Williamson, state of Tennessee, being in feeble health, but of sound and disposing mind and memory, contemplating the uncertainty of life and the certainty of death, do make and ordain, and publish, this my last will and testament, hereby revoking and annulling all former and other wills by me before ordained or published Item, I direct that all my past debts shall be paid.

"Item, I give and bequeath to my beloved sister, Sarah Ann Sims, all my interest in the growing crop on the place where we now reside and also my buggy and harness and the mare and colt. I also give to my sister all that she owes me for borrowed money, both that for which I hold her note and that for which I have not taken any note. I also give and bequeath to my said sister all my stock of cattle and hogs and my farming utensils of every description. Item, I give and bequeath to my beloved niece Ann A. Sims and Marion Sims, infant daughter of my said sister, all my land and negroes my Jack Tallyrand (*sic:* the compiler) and my meaning is to give to my said nieces not only the land for which I have a full and complete title, but I mean to give them all the sight (right? the compiler), title, claim and interest that I have to or for any lands whatever. But it is my will, that the guardian of said children shall have power to sell a certain tract of land, which I own, lying in Haywood county if at any time it may be deemed advisable for the interest of said children. It is also my will that the guardian of said children, may sell any of the negroes, hereby given to them if any of them should hereafter become disobedient and ungovernable.

"It is also my wish that said guardian shall sell Tallyrand at private sale whenever an opportunity offers of getting his value which is to be judged by the guardian.

"Alexander Ewing.

"Witness, Benjamin D. Smith."*

iii Randall McGavock Ewing; legatee in the Will of his father, Captain Alexander Ewing, 1822.

iv William Black Ewing; legatee in the Will of his father, Captain Alexander Ewing; indicated as having a son, William Black Ewing, called grandson in the said Will.

Note: Captain Alexander Ewing, in his Will, mentioned a grandson, Oscar Smith Ewing, without stating which of the testator's sons was father to this child.

v Lucinda Ewing; not mentioned in the Will of Alexander Ewing, but known by the author to have been his daughter; born in Williamson County, Tennessee, December 10, 1792; died April 21, 1848; married, December 18, 1810, James, son of Hugh McGavock; born April 1, 1786, in Wythe County, Virginia; died October 12, 1833; said James and Lucinda (Ewing) McGavock having children:

1 Alexander Ewing McGavock; a legatee in the Will of his grandfather, Captain Alexander Ewing, 1822.

2 Nancy Kent McGavock; a legatee in the said Will of her grandfather.

vi Sarah Ann Ewing; not named in the Will of Captain Alexander Ewing, but called (by her married name of

---

Note by the compiler: Following the copy of this Will is noted: "Recorded in Court House at Franklin, Tennessee." No executor of the Will is named in the said copy, nor, as already mentioned, is any date given, save the above-stated "October 1850" in the heading to this copy.

Sims), sister, in the Will of Alexander Ewing, 1850, who, it is clear, apparently, was Alexander Ewing, Junior, son of Captain Alexander Ewing; married, first, Boyd McNairy Sims; married, second, Joseph W. Carter, who died before the Civil War; married, third, February 16, 1875, Judge John C. Gaut; had children:

1 Ann A. Sims; a legatee in the Will, 1850, of her uncle, Alexander Ewing.

2 Marion Sims; an infant, 1850, when named as a legatee, in the Will of her uncle, Alexander Ewing.

3 Carrie Sims; evidently born after 1850.

The author of the present work on "Leeper-Drake Kith and Kin" has believed that the foregoing Sarah Ann Ewing was either the daughter of Captain Alexander Ewing, or else his granddaughter. But, as above said, the Will of the younger Alexander Ewing, 1850, calling her sister, seems to place her, without question, as a daughter of Captain Alexander. She was probably the youngest child, and not married or of age to be married, when her father made his Will.

One of the daughters of the aforesaid Sarah Ann Ewing (it seems probable born either of her first marriage, to Boyd McNairy Sims, of her second marriage, to Joseph W. Carter), married ——— Richardson.

The author had believed also that the said Sarah Ann Ewing had a brother, Hubbard Ewing. No record, however, has been found of a son of that name in the family of Captain Alexander Ewing. It seems probable that Hubbard Ewing was a grandson of Captain Alexander, or, even, of a still later generation in descent from Captain Alexander.

Hubbard Ewing had the following children:

i Susie Lee Ewing; married, 1883, Winder McGavock; had children: a daughter, who married Haynes Ayers; Winder McGavock, Junior.

ii Sallie Ewing; married ——— Roberts.

iii Doctor Alexander Hubbard Ewing; married, 1906, Gertrude Wallis (whose mother was daughter of Doctor J. S. Park), who died in 1931; had children: Alexander Ewing; Fanny Park Ewing.

Related to this family of Ewing, as being a kinsman of Benjamin Drake and Harriet (Criddle) Smith, was Doctor W. G. Ewing, prominent as a physician in Nashville. He died in 1914. His wife was Elizabeth Overton. She was born, June 9, 1860, at "Travelers' Rest," and was the daughter of Colonel John and Harriet (Maxwell) Overton. Colonel Overton built the famous "Maxwell House" in Nashville, naming it for his wife's family. This, for many years, was a celebrated hostelry of the South, its good cheer heralded far and wide, in modern times, because of the brand of coffee named for it. Elizabeth (Overton) Ewing died December 27, 1931, at her home, "Ravenscroft."

Gambill Family

IN THE PRESENT HISTORY of descendants and kinfolks of Captain James Leeper and Susan Drake, his wife, the records found by the author have now been set down herein, except as to the lineage from Susannah Savannah Smith who married William Frederick Gambill. For clarity, the following data concerning her, though briefly stated above, are repeated. It seemed advisable to the compiler of this work to place the lineage from Susannah Savannah (Smith) Gambill as the last of the lineage relating to the Leeper-Drake Kith and Kin, because it is in this part of such "Kith and Kin" that the present author belongs, through her marriage to Susannah Savannah (Smith) Gambill's son. Some account of the author's own ancestry will be given, following the record of the Gambill family.

Susannah Savannah Smith was the daughter of Benjamin Drake Smith and the latter's wife, Harriet (Criddle) Smith. This daughter was born November 27, 1846. She died in 1877. Her marriage to William Frederick Gambill was solemnized, by Reverend J. W. McDonald, on January 17, 1872. She was the granddaughter of Alexander and Sarah Jane (Leeper) Smith, and the great-granddaughter of Captain James and Susan (Drake) Leeper.

The surname of the Gambill family is variously spelled. Gambell and Gamble seem to have been used more frequently than other forms. The Coat-Armor of the family, resident in Ireland, is blazoned as follows:

Arms—Azure, a fleur-de-lis or.

Crest—A Roman soldier in full costume, proper.

This was, it seems certain, the older form of Arms borne by the family. A blazon, without statement of the family's Seat, gives the same Coat, but with a chief ermine, and, for Crest: a crane, in the beak a rose stalked and leaved proper.

William Frederick Gambill, husband of Susannah Savannah Smith, was the son of William and Ann (Wheless) Gambill. Account of the Wheless family will be given subsequently herein.

It has been thought probable that William Gambill (father of William Frederick Gambill) descended from the family in Augusta County, Virginia, whose surname appears to have been spelled, most frequently, there, Gamble.

Robert Gamble came from Londonderry, Ireland, to Virginia, about 1735. He settled in what was to become Augusta County. This County was formed from part of Orange County, Virginia, in 1745; and Orange was taken off from Spotsylvania County, in 1734. Therefore, if the approximate date of Robert Gamble's coming is correct, he probably lived in what was then either Spotsylvania or Orange.

Robert Gamble brought with him, from Ireland, a son, James Gamble, born in 1729. James married Agnes, sister of Joseph Bell, and they had children: Robert Gamble; John Gamble; Agnes Gamble, who married ——— Davis; Elizabeth Gamble, who married ——— Moffett; and Esther Gamble, who married ——— Bell.

Robert Gamble, the younger, son of James and Agnes (Bell) Gamble, was born in Augusta County, Virginia, September 3, 1754. His education was in an old-time school of the period, named Liberty Hall Academy, and considered of unusual excellence. Soon after becoming of age, and beginning his career as a merchant, the War of the American Revolution was launched. He became the Lieutenant of the first Company raised in Augusta County, for the patriot cause. Advanced to the rank of Captain, he fought in active service throughout the War. Either during the Revolution, or afterwards, he became Major. Robert Gamble took part in many historic battles, and was taken prisoner by the British in South Carolina, being held on a vessel in Charleston Harbour.

Colonel Robert Gamble married Catherine Grattan, daughter of John Grattan, who resided in what became the village of Mount Crawford, Augusta County, On May 17, 1780, Robert Gamble's parents, James and Agnes Gamble, conveyed to him four hundred and twenty acres in the County, next to their own land apparently. On this tract, Colonel Gamble resided, and there his children were born. He had another residence, in Staunton, Augusta County, where, after the War, he and his brother-in-law, Robert Grattan, were merchants in partnership. About 1792, he removed to Richmond, where, says an historian of Augusta County, "he became a prosperous business man and influential citizen." His home in Richmond was on an eminence, named for him, "Gamble's Hill."

On leaving Staunton, and Augusta County, Colonel Gamble sold his farm there to his brother, John Gamble, and it later passed to John's son, William Gamble. Research in Augusta County, Virginia, has not been undertaken to seek the ancestry of William

Gambill, father of William Frederick Gambill (husband of Susannah Savannah Smith); but it seems possible that the said William, son of John, and nephew of Colonel Robert Gamble aforesaid, might, by means of research, be proven identical with William Gambill, father of William Frederick Gambill.

On April 12, 1810, in an accident while riding, Colonel Robert Gamble was thrown from his horse, and died in a short time. High praise was given to him by a contemporary: "He was a faithful soldier of the Revolution, a sincere and zealous Christian, one of the best of fathers, and honestest of men." Waddell, Augusta County's historian, wrote, in his "Annals of Augusta County, of Robert Gamble, as follows:

"His home in Richmond was the seat of an elegant hospitality and within its walls were frequent gatherings of the veterans of the Revolution and others, including Generals Washington and Knox and Chief Justice Marshall. But he did not forget the friends of his early days and native county and by them and their posterity his name and memory have always been revered and cherished."

The brother of Colonel Robert Gamble, as already said, was John Gamble. He also was a patriot in our War for Independence, and attained the rank of Captain. He married Rebecca McPheeters. Her brother was a clergyman, Reverend Doctor McPheeters.

Captain John Gamble died in 1831, on the farm where he was born, which, as already mentioned, was in Augusta County, the home of his parents, James and Agnes (Bell) Gamble, and of his grandparents, or, certainly, of his grandfather, Robert Gamble, First, who came to Virginia from Ireland, bringing his said son, James (as a child), but whose wife may have died before this coming in 1735.

The children of Captain John and Rebecca (McPheeters) Gamble were:

    i James Gamble; became a clergyman.
    ii William Gamble; mentioned above as inheriting from his father land in Augusta County, which had belonged to William's uncle, Colonel Robert Gamble, and had been conveyed to the latter by his parents, James and Agnes Gamble.
    iii Philander Gamble.
    iv Robert Gamble.
    v Theophilus Gamble.

vi Rebecca Gamble; married ——— Ramsey; inherited from her father five hundred acres on Little Muddy Creek in Logan County, Kentucky, evidently a Military Grant, and which was granted to Captain John Gamble on September 15, 1795; had a daughter, Mary J. Ramsey, who appears to have shared in her grandfather's bequest of this land.

vii ——— Gamble; a daughter; married ——— Irvin.

As noted above, it may be that research would show the relationship between the foregoing Gamble family of Augusta County, Virginia, and the family of William Gambill, believed to have been so related, and who, as already stated, married Ann Wheless, and was the father of William Frederick Gambill.

By the marriage of William Frederick Gambill to Susannah Savannah Smith, were born the following children:

i William Wheless Gambill; described subsequently.
ii Harriet Criddle Gambill; described below.

Harriet Criddle Gambill, the daughter of William Frederick and Susannah Savannah (Smith) Gambill, was born August 5, 1874. On July 31, 1897, she married Henleigh Bennett Hunter, who was born September 13, 1873. He was the son of John Henry and Martha (Bennett) Hunter. The said John Henry Hunter was son of Henleigh Stone and Maria (Moore) Hunter. Henleigh Stone Hunter was son of Henry and Jane (Bennett) Hunter.

Mr. and Mrs. Henleigh Bennett reside on their estate, named "Riversmeet," in Williamson County, Tennessee, and on Leeper's Fork, so-called in memory of Captain James Leeper.

Their children are as follows:

i William Wheless Gambill, Junior; described subsequently.
ii Julia Roberta Gambill; described subsequently.
iii Nell Gambill; born November 23, 1902; died December 22, 1902; her resting-place in the McNish family plot, Spring Hill Cemetery.
iv Benjamin Drake Smith Gambill; described subsequently.
i Martha Hunter; born February 12, 1899; married William Farrell; resides in Short Hills, New Jersey; has issue:
1 Martha Farrell; born September 29, 1921.

2 William F. Farrell; born November 22, 1931.

ii Susan Hunter; born March 11, 1903; died November 5, 1913.

iii Harriet Hunter; born May 26, 1905; graduated from Ward-Belmont College, May 28, 1925; married, January 19, 1934, William McCullough; resides in Pittsburgh, Pennsylvania; has a son and a daughter:

 1 William Hunter McCullough; born November 5, 1934.

 2 Ann McCullough; born June 4, 1936.

The first-born child and only son of the above-described William Frederick and Susannah Savannah (Smith) Gambill was, as already stated, William Wheless Gambill. He was born, in Saint Louis, Missouri, on October 8, 1872. His residence was in Nashville, Tennessee, and there he died, August 19, 1933. He was a man of lovable personality, and of high principles and sensitive honour. The present history of the descendant of Captain James Leeper and Susan Drake, his wife, among whom was William Wheless Gambill, is a tribute to him.

On September 22, 1897, in the old First Cumberland Presbyterian Church, on the corner of Fifth Avenue and Commerce Street, in Nashville, Tennessee, by the Reverend Doctor I. D. Steele, were married William Wheless Gambill and Nellie Louise McNish. A history of the McNish and allied families will appear subsequently in the present work.

The children of William Wheless and Nellie Louise (McNish) Gambill are:

William Wheless Gambill, Junior, eldest child of William Wheless and Nellie Louise (McNish) Gambill, was born August 18, 1898, in the old Hillman home, Nashville, Tennessee, on the site of the present Methodist Publishing House, corner of Ninth and Broad Streets. He is President of Gambill Distributing Company, of Nashville. On September 5, 1918, he married Jessie Cornelius. She was born in Mount Eagle, Tennessee, July 21, 1899, the daughter of Benjamin Franklin and Mattie Luanza (Campbell) Cornelius. There follows some account of her ancestry.

Jessie (Cornelius) Gambill is the great-granddaughter of Jesse Cornelius, of Union County, Pennsylvania. He was a miller by occupation, and died on May 31, 1833, as the result of an accident in the machinery of his mill. His son, William Robertson Cornelius, was born in Union County, December 23, 1824. He became the proprietor of a furniture factory in Nashville, Tennessee, located at 49 Spring Street, where now stands the Maxwell House; and, later, also was engaged in the business of Undertaking. During the Civil War, he entered into contract, both with the United States Army and the Confederate Army, to bury, or ship to their homes, the bodies of the soldiers who died in his locality. In all, he performed such service for over thirty-three thousand soldiers. He conducted establishments in this work at Nashville and at Murfreesboro, Tennessee.

William Robertson Cornelius married, in 1850, Martha Dorris; and, in 1900, was celebrated the Golden Anniversary of their wedding.

The aforesaid Benjamin Franklin Cornelius was the son of William Robertson and Martha (Dorris) Cornelius. He was born August 11, 1851, and died January 20, 1926. On February 15, 1877, he married Mattie Luanza Campbell, was the daughter of Reuben and Kitty (Sutphin) Campbell. She was born March 8, 1854, and died September 26, 1929.

The children of William Wheless Gambill, Junior, and his wife Jessie (Cornelius) Gambill are:

    i Cornelia Gambill, born August 29, 1919, at 1006 Nineteenth Avenue, South, Nashville, Tennessee; graduated from Peabody Demonstration School and, also, from Junior College Department of Ward-Belmont. She married September 16, 1939, at home, 2805 Acklen Avenue, Nashville, Tennessee, Lieutenant Robert Worrell Love (now Lieutenant-Colonel), son of Mr. and Mrs. Robert John Love. Lieutenant Love attended Vanderbilt University where he was a member of the Beta Theta Pi Fraternity and was graduated from the United States Military Academy at West Point, New York.

    ii Gloria Gambill, born October 3, 1923, at 2001 Murphy Avenue, Nashville, Tennessee; graduated from Vanderbilt University June, 1945.

    iii Martha Ann Gambill, born July 1, 1930, in Room Number 206, Saint Thomas Hospital.

Julia Roberta Gambill, the second child of William Wheless and Nellie Louise (McNish) Gambill was born on Easter, April 7, 1901.

On May 21, 1918, her marriage was solemnized by the Reverend Mr. Cleveland, minister of the Presbyterian Church at Franklin, Tennessee, to Ellis Camillus Huggins, Junior, who was born December 24, 1900. He was the son of Ellis Camillus and Lena Tate Huggins.

In 1911, Mr. Huggins, Senior, organized, in company with others, the Hermitage Hardware Company, at 309 Third Avenue, North, Nashville. He took active part in the business of this firm until 1925, when it was sold to the Keith-Simmons Hardware Company. While having retired from active commercial affairs about three years before his death, he was, at that period, associated with the Brannan-Huggins Motor Company.

On December 21, 1897, Ellis Camillus Huggins, Senior, married Evalena Tate. She was the daughter of George Samuel and Mary Eliza (Owen) Tate, who were married January 19, 1869. At the time of her death, Mrs. Huggins was Regent of the Cumberland Chapter, Daughters of the American Revolution. She had joined that society through her descent from James Hunter, her great-great-great-grandfather, who was a patriot of our War for Independence.

The Tate lineage of Ellis Camillus Huggins, Junior, husband of Julia Roberts Gambill, has been traced back to James Tate, who married Margaret Nelson. She was the daughter of David and Isabel (Craige) Nelson.

The said first-known Tate ancestor, James Tate, was father of George Tate, who married Nancy Strain. Their son, Alexander J. Tate, married Sarah Bryan. The above-mentioned George Samuel Tate (husband of Mary Owen), was son of Alexander J. and Sarah (Bryan) Tate; and, as already stated, Evalena Tate (wife of Ellis Camillus Huggins, Senior), was the daughter of George Samuel and Mary (Owen) Tate were the parents of Evalena (Tate) Huggins, the mother of Ellis Camillus Huggins, Junior.

The following pedigree is recorded of ancestry of Nancy Strain, who married George Tate, as noted in the foregoing Tate lineage.

Andrew Mitchell married, in Ireland, Mary McGowan. Their son, John Mitchell, married, in North Carolina, Agnes Tate. She was of the same Tate family already described, and whose residence was at Hawfields, in Orange County, North Carolina.

Peggy Mitchell, daughter of the said John and Agnes (Tate) Mitchell, became the wife of David Strain. Their son, Alexander

Strain, married Miriam Hunter. Nancy Strain, wife of George Tate, as set forth in the Tate lineage already given, was the daughter of Alexander and Miriam (Hunter) Strain.

The aforesaid ancestry in the Huggins, Tate, and allied families, has become a part of the heritage of the only child of the above-described Ellis Camillus Huggins, Junior, and his wife, Julia Roberta (Gambill) Huggins. This child is Julia Gambill Huggins. She was born on June 15, 1919, in Nashville, Tennessee, at 1006 Nineteenth Avenue, South, and married, September 10, 1938, Ted Charles Knecht, son of Mr. and Mrs. Oliver Norton Knecht of Trinidad, Colorado.

Dr. Henry Wade Dubose, pastor of Highland Park Presbyterian Church, performed the ceremony which took place at the home of the Bride's parents, Mr. and Mrs. Ellis Huggins, 3920 Woodland Drive, Dallas, Texas.

Records have now been given of the two eldest children of the above-described William Wheless and Nellie Louise (McNish) Gambill. Their third child, Nell Gambill, as already said, died in babyhood.

Their fourth and youngest child is Benjamin Drake Smith Gambill. He was born March 27, 1904. After his graduation from Duncan Preparatory School, he attended Vanderbilt University. He is the President of the Braid Electric Company at Nashville, Tennessee.

On January 15, 1936, Mr. Gambill married Mary Bell Keith Glasgow. The officiating clergyman was the Reverend Thomas Barr, Associate Minister of the First Presbyterian Church of Nashville, and the wedding took place at the Bride's home, "Montrose," on Golf Club Lane, that city.

Mary Bell Keith (Glasgow) Gambill is the daughter of Doctor and Mrs. McPheeters Glasgow, of Nashville. She studied at Wellesley College, and received the Degree of Bachelor of Science from the University of Chicago.

The present history has now recorded all the descendants, as known to the author, of Captain James Leeper and Susan Drake, his wife. Account also has been given of many families allied through marriage to these descendants. There remains to be set forth the ancestry of Nellie Louise (McNish) Gambill, wife of William Wheless Gambill. This will be done in the subsequent

Part II of this book. Immediately following, however, is a sketch of the Wheless family, as written by Edith R. Whitley, after genealogical research on this subject.

Wheless Family

THE WHELESS FAMILY appears, from the rent-rolls of King William County, Virginia, 1704, to have been one of those settling in southeastern Virginia. Joseph Wheless is shown in that year with one hundred and thirty acres of land.

"In 1740, in the Albemarle Parish Register, in Surry and Sussex Counties, Virginia, Thomas Oliver was recorded as Godfather to James, son of Joseph and Mary Wheless.

"Little is known of this family in the early days, before the Revolution.

"In 1790, William Wheless, Jacob 'Whelas,' and Mildred 'Whelas' were living in North Carolina, each the head of a family. Sion and Butson 'Wheelas' were soldiers in the Revolutionary War while living in North Carolina. (North Carolina State and Colonial Records, Volume 17, Page 258).

"Joseph 'Wheelis' went from North Carolina to Tennessee in 1806, and settled in Montgomery County on Brush Creek, where he purchased land from James Perkins, August 20, 1806. (Montgomery County Deed, Book D, Page 308). He was buried there, on the Harvé Bearden farm, about one mile from Hickory Point. I visited this graveyard in 1929, and learned from Mr. Bearden's son that there were two graveyards, not more than half a mile, if quite so far, apart, just across the Creek from each other, the older one being on a hill from the Creek and in a pasture-lot. Some thirty or more graves are there, marked only with small head- and foot-stones, without inscriptions. The only inscribed stone that I have learned about as ever being in this graveyard was that of Joseph Wheeless, born 1760. Some years ago, a storm uprooted a very large tree, which crushed the stone, and, therefore, it is now impossible to obtain a full copy of the inscription. The date of birth was supplied by Mr. Paca, who stated that he well remembered the birth-date, but did not recall the date of death of Joseph Wheless. Mr. Paca also stated that the grave by the side of that of Joseph Wheless was that of the latter's wife, Mary.

"Acquilla (Aquila? the compiler) Wheless owned the home after his father, Joseph. This Acquilla was Sheriff of Montgomery County for a number of years. Mr. Paca stated that he, himself, had owned the farm for about forty years, and that there had never been any burials there, since he purchased the land.

"I was told that a Joseph Wheless, father of Joseph (Punk) Wheless, was buried in this cemetery. Miss Nellie Wheless was the last of the family to live in the old Wheless house, and she was buried there. Acquilla Wheless sold it to Jacke (*sic*: the compiler) Hogan. The Hogan and Wheless families were related.

"Another graveyard, known as the Stewart graveyard, and in which members of both the Wheless and Hogan families were buried, is only a short way from the first one herein mentioned. This farm is now owned by Mr. Carney Lyle of Clarksville. At the Hogan-Wheless graveyard (the Stewart graveyard? the compiler), I copied the following:

John Hogan born 1778 died 1878.

Mary Hogan born 1774 died 1877.

There were other tombstones, but none bearing the names, Hogan or Wheless, that I found. This Hogan graveyard is on McAdoo's Creek. Mr. Graham, who lived near the place, made the statement that he thought the name on the above-mentioned stone was Martha Hogan, and not Mary Hogan.

"The old Wheless house is located about one mile southwest of Hickory Point, Tennessee, Post Office, and about twelve miles south of Clarksville. It is owned by H. M. Bearden, and is occupied by a Mr. Graham, who is in some way connected with the Wheless family. It is the original house on Brush Creek, about one hundred yards from the main Big Brush Creek. Originally, there were three rooms and a hall in the house, but there are only two rooms now. The oldest one known to have lived in this house by the Graham boys was Miss Nellie Wheless. This house was built of poplar logs, chinked and daubed, now weather-boarded with poplar weather-board, and now sealed with poplar sealing, very much wealthered. The old rock chimney still stands and is in use. A new roof has replaced the old one. There is a spring about one hundred yards from the house, which supplies the water. The old barns, smoke-house, and cribs are standing, and were made of poplar logs, which are much weather-worn, showing them to be very old. The land is worn and washed very badly about the house, excepting in the yard.

"Acquilla Wheless, mentioned above, was the father of Joseph Wheless, who died in St. Louis about 1905. His wife was Ellen Thomas Malone, of Athens, Alabama. Acquilla was an intimate of

Andrew Jackson. They had a silver cane, engraved, 'Our Stick,' followed by their names.

"Wesley Wheless, who built 'the Wheless Place,' ——— a forty-room, castellated mansion, just across 'Confederate Hill,' in East Nashville, ——— was a brother of Joseph. This old mansion burned in 1887.

"John F. Wheless, born in Montgomery County, Tennessee, February 3rd, 1839, was a brother of Wesley and Joseph. They were sons of Acquilla Wheless and his wife, Mary Hogan, who were married in Montgomery County in 1820, and died there about 1846. The elder Joseph Wheless died in 1844, having been born in 1760.

"Wesley Wheless married Sarah Ann Hobson, of Nashville, Tennessee. They were parents of Hobson Wheless."

Part II
ANCESTRY AND KINDRED OF
NELL McNISH GAMBILL, WIFE OF
WILLIAM WHELESS GAMBILL

McNish

THIS FAMILY is one of those ancient houses of Scotland, of Celtic origin, and probably descended from ancestry which, in the Fifth Century, overran part of Caledonia, and gave their own name of Scot to the land. After the Romans, who had not been able to conquer the Native Picts of what now is Scotland, withdrew from Britain, in the year 410 A. D., the Scots from Ireland, the Welsh, and, soon, the Anglo-Saxon invaders of Britain, all sought to establish themselves in the northern part of the island. Soon, also, the Scandinavian Vikings made raids, particularly on the islands off the coast of Scotland. But it was the Scots, as the Irish then were called, who secured the firmest hold on Caledonia, and made it Scotland.

One of the families or Clans considered of this Celtic origin in Scotland is that of Gregor, or MacGregor. The beginnings of its history are lost in the mists of the centuries, but it has always believed itself to be of Royal blood. Of this Clan, it is said in "The Scottish Clans and Their Tartans," published in Edinburgh and London, by W. and A. K. Johnston, the Ninth Edition of which standard work was published in 1907, as follows:

"This is a clan of ancient lineage, and who, according to their motto, " 'S Rioghail mo dhream" ('Royal is my race'), claim royal descent."

To this clan belonged the famous "Rob Roy," immortalized by Sir Walter Scott. He was "Rob" MacGregor, born in 1671, and who died in 1734. His soubriquet of "Roy" came from his red hair. In 1693, though by no means the direct heir, he was made Chief of the Clan. Later, evicted by debt from his estates, by the Duke of Montrose, from which he had borrowed largely, Rob Roy became an outlaw. Finally, he made his peace with the Duke, and, though for a while imprisoned in England, was pardoned, in 1727, and returned to Scotland. The characteristic of the MacGregors is a bold, confident courage. As an old song describes their valiant bearing, even through misfortunes, "MacGregor, despite them, shall flourish forever!" And their habit of leadership is expressed in the proverbial saying that, "Where MacGregor is, there is the head of the table!" The Clan's traditional Badge, the Pine-Tree, symbolizes the strong, reliant, unbending persistence and vigor of the race.

David MacNish and William A. Tod, authors of "The History of the Clan Neish or MacNish," state that "the Clan Neish were also know as MacIlduys at an early period. MacIlduy or Mac-gille-duibh was probably the cognomen of one of the early chiefs of the Neish clan." These authors question the fact that the MacNish (which never has been considered by authorities a Clan itself), which, as they correctly say, is connected with MacIlduy, was derived from the aforesaid great Clan of MacGregor. But this derivation, both for MacNish and MacIlduy, is definitely stated, by Frank Adam, F. S. A., Scot., in his excellent book, published by the aforesaid W. and A. K. Johnston, Edinburgh and London, 1896, "What Is My Tartan?" A study of the Coat-Armor, borne by the families, bears out this statement.

As is true of nearly all Scottish surnames of Celtic origin, the name of MacNish is found variously spelled. The endeavors, at different periods, to reconcile the old Celtic forms and the modern English forms is doubtless the reason for this.

Besides MacNish and MacNeish, MacNeath, Naish, and Ness, are among orthographies followed, of which there are several more.

Probably the oldest form of the Coat-Armor is the following:

Azure, a chevron between two mullets in chief and a crescent in base argent.

The fact that this Coat-of-Arms is without Crest indicates that the family bore Arms prior to the introduction of Crests in European heraldry, which, in Britain, was about the middle of the Twelve Hundreds.

Similar Arms, somewhat elaborated from the blazon just given, have a Crest: a dexter hand holding a sword in pale proper. This is blazoned in Burke's General Armory (the generally accepted authority for English and Scottish Arms), under the name, Naish. Burke blazons the ancient form, described above, under MacNeish, — "M'Neish," — MacNeath, — "M'Neath," — and gives a still simpler form, under Ness, with a Crest. This blazon follows.

Arms — Argent, three chevrons sable (which, correctly, would be three chevronels, — narrow chevrons).

Crest — A dexter hand holding a laurel branch proper.

The sword and the raised arm are characteristics of the Mac-Gregor Arms. Another characteristic of these Arms is the use of the oak. Fairbairns' "Family Crests" gives, for the Crest of M'Nish: An arm, embowed and couped in fess proper, vested azure, holding an oak-sprig vert fructed or. Fairbairns also gives another Crest, for M'Nish: An eagle rising proper. This, however, is unusual. It appears to have been used by a branch of the family in modern times, with the modern Motto: *Anima non astutia.* No ancient Motto has been found as used by the MacNish family. Possibly, they used the old Motto of MacGregor: "E'en do, bait spair nocht." Or, it may be, that the MacNish descendants of the Clan MacGregor used the very old Motto, quoted above: " 'S Rioghail mo dhream" — "Royal is my race."

Although the use of Mottoes in heraldry goes back to a very remote period, their origin being the battle-cries of the early ancestors, the Motto in Arms is not considered a fixed and unchangeable part of Coat-Armor. It is regarded more or less, as an individual feature in heraldry, and it is correct, according to all accepted authorities, for a family, — or a member of a family, — to use, alter, or discard the Motto. Perhaps, the recommended form of Coat-Armor for the MacNish family of America might be blazoned thus:

Arms — Azure, a chevron between two mullets in chief and a crescent in base argent.

Motto — Royal is my race.

So far as can be stated, without undertaking extensive research abroad, and in accordance with the aforesaid authority on the Clans of Scotland, Frank Adam, F. S. A., Scot., the family of McNish was a Sept or branch of the MacGregor Clan. As already noted, also, this relationship to the MacGregors is confirmed by study of the Coat-Armor of both families.

The first known ancestor in the McNish lineage herein presented was David McNish, who was a native of Virginia. Dates of his birth and death have not been learned; but it appears probable that he was born about the Seventeen Seventies. He had a grandson (William Dean McNish, to be described subsequently), born in 1826, which fixed date indicates the probable period of David McNish's birth.

David McNish married Elizabeth Lewis, also a Virginian. Her paternal ancestry is thought to be the family of John Lewis, the famous pioneer in what was to become Augusta County, Virginia. This, however, is not claimed, by the author of "Leeper-Drake Kith and Kin," to be based on actual evidence. Nevertheless, tradition is not to be despised. Neither does the present author claim more than the weight of tradition for the statement that Elizabeth Lewis, wife of David McNish, was related to, or descended from, that member of the Lewis family (his first name unknown), who married Mary, daughter of Captain Charles and Hannah (Innes) Brent. Account of the Brent and Innes families follows.

The Brents of Virginia derived from the Brent family of Cossington, in Somersetshire, England. George Brent of Cossington married Marianna, daughter of Sir John Peyton, of Doddington, Isle of Ely. A brother of George Brent was Admiral Giles Brent, who was Governor of Maryland, 1643.

The Coat-Armor of this family is blazoned:

Arms — Gules, a wyvern argent.

Crest — A wyvern's head between two wings expanded argent.

Motto — Silentio et diligentia ("By silence and diligence")

The said George and Marianna (Peyton) Brent were the parents of George Brent, Junior, who was their sixth son. Like many other younger sons of old English families, he emigrated to America, settling, in 1660, in what, four years later, was to become Stafford County, Virginia, but which, in 1660, was part of Westmoreland County. George Brent had two estates in this part of the Colony: Woodstock and Brenton, as he named them. In 1670, he was made Captain of a Troop of Horse. In 1683, Captain Brent was appointed to be Receiver-General, North of the Rappahannock River.

Captain George Brent married twice. His first wife was Elizabeth, daughter of Captain William Green, whose wife was a sister of Sir William Layton. His second marriage took place on March 27, 1687 (or 1688), when he espoused ——— Sewell, daughter of Henry Sewell and the latter's wife, who, at the time of her daughter's marriage to Captain Brent, had married for her second husband Lord Baltimore.

Captain George Brent and his first wife, Elizabeth (Green) Brent, had issue:

    i George Brent.

    ii Nicholas Brent.
    iii Robert Brent; described presently.
    iv Marianne Brent.
    v Elizabeth Brent.

Robert Brent, third son of the preceding Captain George and Elizabeth (Green) Brent, has been described as "a prominent, influential citizen of affairs." He resided at Woodstock, his estate in Stafford County. On July 8, 1702, he married Susannah Seymour, daughter of Captain David Seymour, who, in turn, was son of Florentine Seymour, Governor of Bermuda, who died in Virginia.

Robert and Susannah (Seymour) Brent had two sons:
    i George Brent; described presently.
    ii Robert Brent: born in 1705; died in 1750; married, 1732, Mary Wharton, who was born in 1706, died January 1, 1774, and was the daughter of Henry and Jane (Doyne) Wharton.

George Brent, son of Robert and Susannah (Seymour) Brent, was born in 1703. He lived on the family estate, Woodstock, in Stafford County, Virginia, and "took a prominent and active part in affairs of the Colony." In 1730, he married Mary Firmingham, of Bermuda.

The children of George and Mary (Firmingham) Brent were:
    i Charles Brent, described presently.
    ii Thomas Brent.
    iii George Brent.
    iv Judith Brent (perhaps married ——— King).
    v Amy Brent (perhaps married ——— Haines).
    vi Lucy Brent.

Captain Charles Brent, the eldest son of George and Mary (Firmingham) Brent, was born about 1735. He was a patriot in the stormy period preceding and during the War for our Independence, and, in consequence, his home was burned by the Tory troops under Lord Dunmore, then Governor of Virginia, this outrage taking place in 1776.

The wife of Captain Charles Brent was Hannah Innes. She is said to have been either the daughter or granddaughter of Reverend Hugh Innes, a clergyman of the Anglican Established Church, and who was a native of Scotland. This Innes family is said to descend from Sir Robert Innes, who married Grizel Stewart. She was daughter to James Stewart, second Earl of Moray, and the latter's wife, Lady Elizabeth Stewart. Through this marriage, came descent from the Royal Stewart House of Scotland.

The children of Captain Charles and Hannah (Innes) Brent were:

> i Charles Brent; married Ann Gunnell, of Fairfax County, Virginia.

HORATIO MCNISH

- ii Hugh Brent; resided in Paris, Bourbon County, Kentucky; married Elizabeth Baxter.
- iii William Brent.
- iv Mary Brent; married ——— Lewis, and, as has been noted, above herein, is thought to have been ancestress of Elizabeth Lewis, the wife of David McNish.
- v Nancy Brent: married ——— Atwell.
- vi Katherine Brent; married ——— Wrenn.
- vii George Brent; married ——— Wilson, whose father was Doctor ——— Wilson, of Martinsburg, Virginia.

The above-mentioned David McNish (earliest-known ancestor of the McNish lineage herein set forth), and his wife, Elizabeth (Lewis) McNish, were parents of Horatio McNish.

Horatio McNish removed, about 1827, from Virginia to Tennessee and settled at Brentwood. He soon built a two-story Colonial home on the top of a hill just off the Franklin Pike, where, he lived and raised a large family.

Horatio McNish married, in Virginia, about 1818, Susan Dean, an account of whose family will be subsequently given.

The children of Horatio and Susan (Dean) McNish follow:

- i Mary McNish; married James Carsey, described later.
- ii Elizabeth (Betty) Lewis McNish, described subsequently.
- iii Thomas McNish; twin with Lou McNish; died unmarried.
- iv Lou McNish; twin with Thomas McNish.
- v James McNish; born in 1870; married, late in life, Lulu Beech, of Williamson County, Tennessee; had a daughter, Susie Beech, who married Joseph Glenn.
- vi Maria McNish; married Eli Waters, of Williamson County; had a daughter, May Waters, who married James Burnet, and had a daughter, Daisy Burnet, who married Allen Beech and had children: Mildred, who graduated from Trousdale County (Tennessee) High School in 1932; and Milton.
- vii Sarah Virginia McNish; married Thomas E. Fulgham. The following inscriptions give the names of his mother and father and are to be found on the stones in the old

burial ground near Huntsville, Alabama, on the plantation which was originally their home:

Jane McWhirter Fulgham, Born Abbeville District, South Carolina, Died Madison County, Alabama, May 22, 1864; "God giveth his beloved sleep."

James Fulgham, Born in W. Virginia, September 22, 1809, Died 1873; "Blessed are the dead who die in the Lord. They rest from their labor and their works do follow them."

Lillian Fulgham, daughter of Thomas E. and Sarah McNish Fulgham married Thomas James Waggoner, son of Mr. and Mrs. James Waggoner.

 viii William Dean McNish; described subsequently.

 ix Joseph McNish; served during the Civil War as a member of Company B (Rock City Guards), under Colonel Manly; killed at Perryville, Kentucky, October 8, 1862.

 x (Perhaps) Susan Dean McNish.

Mary McNish, daughter of Horatio and Susan (Dean) McNish, married James Carsey, a tobacco merchant. Their children were as follows:

 i William H. Carsey; of whom subsequently.

 ii Eugene Carsey; married Alice Herman, daughter of Doctor Herman, of Nashville, Tennessee; children:

  1 Herman Carsey; married, in 1901, Lottie Gholsen, of Clarksville; have son, Eugene Carsey.

  2 Eugene Carsey; died young; buried at Cave Hill Cemetery, Louisville, Kentucky.

  3 Edwin Carsey, married, November 24, 1917, at Lexington, Kentucky, Katheryn Howard Sprake, daughter of Mrs. N. O. Sprake.

 iii Thomas Carsey; married Mollie Bustard; had several sons,. one, James T. (Zeke) Carsey, was Mascot of Company A, First Tennessee Regiment, at age of thirteen years; married and has daughters, Alma, Marie and Evelyn.

 iv Hal Carsey; married Fannie Wilkerson; children: Elmer Carsey, and Willie Carsey; resided in California where Elmer Carsey and his father both died.

v Sue Carsey; married, first, Elisha Wherry; second, James Beach, of Williamson County, Tennessee.

The grandmother of the said Elisha Wherry was Celia Griffith Cain, of North Carolina, a stone over her grave being marked as follows:

"Celia Griffith Cain, born in Chatham County, North Carolina. Died in Nashville, Tennessee, February 5, 1868, aged one hundred years."

The children of Sue Carsey, by her first husband, were:

1 James Wherry; married; had one son, Carl Wherry.

2 Georgie Wherry; born September 22, 1862; died July 22, 1863.

3 Cora Wherry; married James B. Pope, who died in New York City, July 20, 1930; children:

i James Bolling Pope; born May 12, 1886; died March 29, 1888.

ii Susanne Pope; married Robert Kenyon; Cora Wherry Pope died July 30, 1938.

William H. Carsey, son of James M. and Mary (McNish) Carsey, was born in Franklin, Tennessee, July 9, 1846, and died April 7, 1918. He attended public schools in Nashville, later enrolling in Emory and Henry College, in Virginia. After leaving school he engaged in the wholesale cotton and tobacco business in which he continued until his death.

He was for many years associated with Dortch, Carsey & Co., of Nashville, and prior to that he was associated, for some time, with his father, James M. Carsey. He achieved substantial success in life and no man in the community was more highly esteemed for his integrity and sterling worth.

William H. Carsey married, in 1871, Lee James Calcote, daughter of Lee James and Elizabeth (Overton) Calcote. Elizabeth Overton was a native of Tennessee. A great-great-uncle of Lee James (Calcote) Carsey was Judge John Overton, one time law partner of Andrew Jackson, and his second when Jackson participated in the duel which has gone down in history. The grandparents of Mrs. Carsey were Doctor James and Eliza Henry (Dixon) Overton, the grandmother being a daughter of Tallman Dixon, born in 1756, and his wife, Polly Don Carlos, who was born in 1767. Tallman Dixon was a Major in the Army during the Revolutionary War. His land grant covered what is now Dixon Springs, Smith County, Tennessee. Major Dixon first served as a Lieutenant and received that commission in the 15th of November, 1775. He was promoted to the rank of Major in the First North Carolina Regiment, commanded by Colonel Thomas Clark, February 5, 1777. On January 1, 1783, he was rendered supernumerary.

Lee James Calcote, wife of William H. Carsey, received her education at St. Cecelia Convent, in Nashville. She was a woman of much culture and refinement; was socially prominent, and her beautiful home at 417 Madison Street, Clarksville, Tennessee, afforded most generous hospitality to her host of friends. She was a charter member of the Clarksville chapter of the Daughters of the American Revolution.

The children of William H. and Lee James (Calcote) Carsey were:

    i Willie Lee Carsey; married W. S. Pointdexter; has a daughter, Willie Lee Carsey, who married, December

JULIA STUMP — *Wife of W. D. M Nish*

WILLIAM DEAN McNISH

27, 1930, at the Trinity Episcopal Church, Clarksville, Tennessee, Frederick Victor Brandt.

ii James M. Carsey; married Juanita Anderson; has daughters, Elizabeth Lee Carsey and Juanita Carsey.

iii Overton Carsey; commissioned Second Lieutenant of Infantry, May 28, 1906, in Tennessee National Guard; served on Mexican border; also served with One Hundred Fifteenth Field Artillery, Thirtieth Division, and participated in major engagements of World War.

William Dean McNish, son of Horatio and Susan (Dean) McNish, was born January 6, 1826, and died March 2, 1896. He was living on what is now Greenwood Avenue, in East Nashville, Tennessee, during the Civil War, but he and his family were forced to leave when the town was taken by the Union troops.

A few years ago a picture and an article concerning the McNish homestead appeared with comments on its architectural beauty as follows: "Distinct in charm is this house. A beautiful simplicity note is struck and French farm style is achieved. A sturdy grace characterizes the doorway. At the right a magnolia's rich color contrasts with the green of the shutters on white clap-board." This residence was built for the McNish family by the architect, Tobias Brown. The magnolia tree mentioned in the article was planted by Mrs. McNish, wife of William Dean McNish.

During the Civil War the family suffered great losses and their home was one of the things which they had to sacrifice. While the McNish family were absent in Georgia the house was invaded by Union soldiers, some of whom thrust their bayonets through the family portraits, which the family had valued so highly, and, before leaving, set fire to the house. Very fortunately, however, a friendly neighbor, Mrs. Hunter, had sent an old colored woman to do the family washing and she had left several tubs of water. Seeing the soldiers leave, Mrs. Hunter promptly sent the colored woman back to the house to estimate the damage done, and, finding the house on fire, she soon extinguished the flames with the water from the tubs.

For many years William Dean McNish was postmaster at Nashville.

Following is an article by John C. Cooke in the Nashville Banner, which concerns his activities and contains much interesting general information.

"REMINISCENCES OF NASHVILLE'S OLDEST NEWSPAPER MAN"

"Do you, gentle reader, happen to remember anything of those Civil War days of the early sixties, '61 to '65, and on through the nightmare of reconstruction? To this late hour of my life I trace impressions left by the recollections of those hectic times that tried the souls of men as they were never tried before, and let us hope we will never be subjected to such a test again. Those days never return, but the recollection of them brings a gloom from the haunting memory of conditions that to the present generation would be accepted as an improbable story. They were troublesome days and the people of the South were hampered and annoyed by the invaders in every way that meanness could devise. But that is a matter not altogether pertinent to this story, which has to do with the difficulty that the home folks experienced in communicating with their relatives and friends in the Confederate Army and those north of the Mason and Dixon Line.

"Mail facilities, of course, were entirely cut off and many tricks were adopted to overcome the restrictions. One was a rather risky expediency of intrusting to spies. A distinguished Confederate would come into the city, gather as many letters as he could, conveniently, and by avoiding the pickets would return to the Army loaded down with letters for the soldiers.

"The late Judge John C. Ferriss told me that on one occasion he carried nearly one thousand letters to Bragg's Army when it was encamped at Tullahoma. Not a few of these were from women and girls. It would be hard to calculate the number of letters carried out by the Misses Fannie and Sallie Battle, sisters; Miss Molly Overall, of Triune; Miss King, of Flatrock, and other ladies who made many trips between Nashville and Bragg's Army. Sam Davis, immortal Boy Scout, probably carried as many, and Dee Job and Tobe Joslin were in Nashville every few days mingling with the soldiers. Many hundreds of letters must have been intrusted to them for delivery to the Confederate boys.

"It may not be generally known that the first Confederate postage stamps ever issued were printed in Nashville at the instance of W. D. McNish somewhere about the last of June, 1861. A Nashville engraver made the plates. At the time James T. Bell was publishing the Nashville Gazette, a red hot Confederate sheet, and like all daily newspaper owners in those days, he operated a job printing shop in connection with his daily paper. The McNish stamps were printed in that office.

"McNish, at different times, was Postmaster at Nashville under the administration both of President Lincoln and President Jefferson Davis. That also is a bit of unwritten history. That was in 1861. Another bit of history is found in the fact that John Lellyett was appointed Postmaster in March, 1862. He served about six months, when he was removed by Andrew Johnson, Military Governor of Tennessee, who appointed A.V.S. Lindsley in his stead. At that time the Federal letters for the soldiers being in excess of 12,000.

"The Nashville Post-Office has occupied its present quarters, at Broadway and Eighth Avenue, for fifty years, or since March, 1882. It had formerly occupied a building at Cedar and Cherry (now Fourth Avenue) streets. Doctor W. P. Jones was Postmaster at the time of the removal to its present location in the Custom House Building. The corner-stone of that building was laid in 1877 with appropriate ceremonies. President Hayes was the guest of the Citizens of Nashville at the time and assisted in laying the Corner-stone.

"The Nashville office became a presidential Post-office in 1836, during the Administration of Robert Armstrong as Postmaster. He held the office for sixteen years, resigning to be consul at Liverpool, to which he was appointed by President James K. Polk. The Civil War history of the Post-office affords an interesting chapter and closely identified with those stirring days. On June 6, 1861, W. D. McNish, who was then Postmaster at Nashville, received orders from Washington to forward all mail directed to points in the seceding states to the dead-letter office at Washington. McNish declined to do this and resigned as Postmaster of the United States. His reasons for taking this step were that he could not conscientiously obey the order from Washington, as much of this mail was from women of the South to their husbands, brothers, sons, and sweethearts, then serving in the army, but from that time forward it was a confederate Post-office. He held the office for about six months, without bond, and was then appointed to the Postmastership by the Confederate Government, a position held by him until the evacuation of Nashville by the Confederate authorities. This was immediately following the fall of Fort Donelson.

"In these distressing times United States postage stamps were of no use here or elsewhere in the South, and as the Confederate Government had not issued any, it was no little trouble to get letters through since it was necessary to prepay them with money. At that time, Dan Adams was an engraver here and Mr. McNish employed him to make three plates for the new stamps for his office, three, five, and ten cents. They were put on sale the latter part of June, 1861, but soon ceased to be of use, as the Confederate Government began to issue stamps about this time. The three-cent stamp was used for newspaper postage, the five-cent stamp for single letters for a distance under five hundred miles, and the ten-cent stamp for any distance exceeding five hundred miles. Only one die was made for each value and they were printed at the Gazette job printing office in Nashville.

"When the Federal troops came to Nashville Mr. McNish had all his office effects sent him at Washington, Georgia, but in order to prevent their capture by Federal troops, the train was blown up between Atlanta and Griffen, and the dies and all the rest were destroyed. Later, Mr. McNish received letters from all parts of the World asking for specimens of the stamps, some of them offering large sums of money for the set of them, but, of course, he could not comply. Maybe some of them are in the keeping of Nashville families today. A few sheets of each of the series would command a fortune.

"When the United States Post-office was suspended there was no mail communication between the North and South, but Louisville, Kentucky, being 'in the Union' still had many persons in Nashville and points further South having friends in the North with whom they wished to correspond, consequently, the American Letter Express was founded at Nashville for the purpose of forwarding mail from this point to Louisville. The plan was about like this: A person desiring to write anyone in the North was required to inclose the letter to be forwarded, with ten cents in money to be inclosed in a second envelope addressed to the American Letter Express, at Nashville, and prepaid by Confederate stamps; the express company would then remove the outer covering and, securing its fee, forwarded the letter to Louisville and it was there mailed, the stamped envelope paying the postage. The express company kept stamped envelopes for sale at Louisville for the use of patrons.

"Pictures of the stamps made with the name of W. D. McNish on them appear on page fifty-eight of the Standard Postage Stamp Catalogue Company, Ltd., New York, 1923, made in different colors.

10c green, worth $400.00, in 1923.
3c carmine, worth $10.00, in 1923.
5c carmine, worth $20.00, in 1923.
5c brick red, worth $20.00, in 1923.
5c gray, worth $30.00, in 1923.
5c violet brown, worth $35.00.

"From excerpts from Nashville newspapers we learn that the Nashville Post Office is older than the State of Tennessee, having been founded April 1, 1796, two months before Tennessee became a State on that date, the President made Nashville a Post Office and appointed Captain John (Black Jack) Gordon, the first Postmaster. Mail was received from Philadelphia via Knoxville, on horse-back, and then shortly afterward the route was extended over the Natchez Trace southwards to New Orleans, through the perils of wilderness, infested by hostile Indians, robbers, and wild animals. At that time the population of Nashville was about four hundred persons.

William and Robert Stothart were next appointed as Postmasters and were followed by Robert B. Curry who served twenty-four years.

Before his successor, John P. Irwin, a nephew of Henry Clay, was appointed, Congressman Sam Houston (who afterwards freed Texas), at that time Democratic Congressman from Nashville, and backer of Mr. Curry, fought a duel in Kentucky over the Postmastership with William White. Houston wounded the gallant Mr. White who had fired his gun at a cloud.

President of the United States and selected Robert Armstrong as Irwin's successor. After Mr. Armstrong, Colonel P. Cheatham, Doctor P. Shelby, William D. McNish, and S. R. Anderson, were successively appointed to the post. It was during the term of Mr. Anderson on June 10, 1861, that the Post Office was closed on account of the Civil War, and eight months later opened by Mr. John Lellyet who did not hold the office long, as one morning in June, 1862, Military Governor Andrew Johnson, out for an early morning walk, discovered that the stage-coach, carrying mail entered eastward via Lebanon, was named for General U. S. Grant, of the Union Army. This was too much for the Governor, who, evidently, considered disrespect to Grant was intended, released Mr. Lellyet "on the spot." Mr. Johnson would have no Rebel sympathizers handling the mail, so he selected Mr. A. V. S. Lindsey, a loyal Republican Union man, who served five years. Mr. Lindsey was succeeded by Judge Bowling Embry, then by Major Hopkins, Colonel William F. Prosser, and Hermon Hasslock, successively. Mr. Hasslock was appointed by President Grant as a reward for a favor. Before the war Mr. Grant was hauling wood near his home in Illinois and once, when his wagon broke down in front of Mr. Hasslock's home, Mr. Hasslock supplied Grant with a new wheel. Mr. Grant thanked him by saying he hoped to be able to return the favor some day, and twenty-five years later did so when he appointed Mr. Hasslock to the Postmastership at Nashville.

Among the later Postmasters of Nashville have been Doctor William Jones; and General B. F. Cheatham, who was succeeded upon his death by his wife,—the only woman to serve as Postmaster of Nashville. Later, came Major Wills, Captain H. J. Cheney, E. S. (General Gene) Shannon, Charles M. McCabe, who advertised Postal service as a means to an end for better service, and Doctor W. J. O'Callighan, who has been successed by Mr. O. F. Minton.

William Dean McNish married, December 14, 1852, the ceremony being performed by the Reverend Jesse B. Ferguson, in Nashville,

Tennessee, Julia Ann Stump, an account of whose family will be given subsequently.

Children of William Dean and Julia Ann (Stump) McNish:
 i   Thomas Horatio McNish; described subsequently.
 ii Hugh Lawson McNish; described subsequently.
 iii Samuel Anderson McNish; described subsequently.
 iv Roberta Lee McNish; described subsequently.
 v   John Joseph McNish; born February 17, 1868; died at Paducah, Kentucky, June 7, 1927; inventor of labor-saving devices for railroads; married Lou Robertson, of Paducah, Kentucky.
 vi James Harold McNish; born August 6, 1870; married Elsie Griffith, who died at San Louis Obispo, California, January 23, 1922, daughter of Horatio and Emma (Wall) Griffith, a Welsh lawyer of Cheyenne, Wyoming; had children: Edward McNish, who married and had one child; Richard McNish, born May 7, 1927; and Margaret Louise McNish; died May 25, 1929; married at Riverside, California, Sunday, April 25, 1927, Rupert M. Hendricks.
 vii William Watson McNish; born May 23, 1859; died January 29, 1895; member of Hamilton, Puryear and McNish, furniture dealers; married Nettie Hargrave; had children: Rowena McNish, who died young, and William Dean McNish, unmarried.
 viii Nellie Louise McNish, described subsequently.

Thomas Horatio McNish, son of William Dean and Julia Ann (Stump) McNish, was born April 14, 1855, and died at Orlando, Florida, January 8, 1933.

Recollections of his early life, particularly during the time of the Civil War, were related by him, late in life, and as they were put in writing and saved we are able to give them here.

"In June, 1862, father (William Dean McNish), who had been driven out of Nashville by Federal troops, wrote to mother to meet him at Columbia, and mother, who was staying at Mr. Owens', near Brentwood, bought an old reliable horse and covered spring wagon, and took three of her children, Hugh, Samuel, and myself, with her, leaving Willie with his Aunt, Mrs. Wat Owen. She took all she could carry with her, not knowing where she would go or what she would need, and started. We spent the first night away at Mr. Stannis' on Big Harpeth River, and the next morning, in fording the river, we stalled in mid-stream. Fortunately, mother was able to employ some negro men to get the wagon across the river and, having some silver change, mixed with a few gold dollars, in paying them she mistook several of the dollars for five and ten-cent silver pieces. Expensive ferrying, I say.

"The next morning we pushed on toward Columbia and near Springhill we were halted by some Confederate soldiers who had decided that mother was a Union spy. Mother did her best to disabuse their minds of the idea, but to no good. She argued that no woman would start out as a spy encumbered with three children and a load of baggage. They were as adamant and started with her to head-quarters, but just in the nick of time, two soldiers with whom she was acquainted happened to come up and we had no further trouble on that score, for they not only did not take her to head-quarters, but sent two soldiers to escort her to Columbia where we met father and with many new experiences we spent two years in the South.

"Mother had quite a lot of Nashville newspapers which she gave to the soldiers and the men simply devoured their contents, for you see they were home papers and they were wild for news from home. If the Federals could have caught her giving them to the soldiers they might have well said she was a spy. But that idea never entered her head. She was for putting distance between herself and the Yankees.

"I have often heard my mother tell how the first "Pickets" told her they would let her pass, but the next ones would stop her saying, "that women played the devil sometimes as well as the men."

"And about the wheel passing over her band-box (containing her treasured poke-bonnet) when it rolled out of the wagon as they were pulling up a steep muddy bank after being mired in mid-stream. (At this juncture she met a friend who had just left my father, and he kindly turned back and lead her to him).

"All three of the boys had to ride in front with her as the big cedar chest which held their belongings completely filled the back of the wagon. This necessitated her holding the youngest boy in front of her between her knees. He was bothered so by the horse's tail switching him in the face that she was compelled to stop at a farm house and borrow a pair of shears with which she proceeded to cut off the tail.

"She left Willie with his aunt, Mrs. Wat Owen, and one night, having extra company, she had to put him on a pallet. He told her, 'You make out like you love me so, and put me on the hard floor to sleep.'

"Mother had a message from Columbia from father saying he had the small-pox, and she did not hear again for several weeks. Then word came for her to join him. He told her in ten minutes after it was known he had the small-pox, everyone vacated the hotel and he had it all to himself. Someone kindly carried his meals to the head of the steps. Fortunately, he had a light case called 'variloid.' From Columbia, they proceeded South to Georgia."

Mr. W. W. Walker, of Lewisburg, Tennessee, has related an incident concerning Thomas McNish, when McNish was but a youth with his family in Georgia. On the ninth of May, 1865, one month after General Lee surrendered, Dibrell's Brigade of Tennessee Cavalry stacked arms to the Federal General Wilson, at Washington. The Federals, after looking over the stacked arms, saw there were but few side arms surrendered and an order was issued by the commander to bring up the pistols. This, however, was not obeyed, and a second order was sent around that if the side arms were not brought up the men would be searched. This had its effect. Mr. Walker had a Colt's army pistol that had been his constant companion and "best friend" for sometime and this he disliked to surrender. Later, while strolling down along a little creek near camp, probably watering his horse, he met a little boy of seven or eight years of age, whose bright, intelligent face attracted him. He soon learned that the boy was a refugee from Nashville with his family and that his name was McNish. Mr. Walker told him about the pistol he prized so highly and how he would have to surrender it to the Federals if he could find no way to dispose of it so that he could get it back in his possession. He felt he could trust the boy, so he gave him his name, home address, regiment, etc., and told him where he would hide the gun under an old log and requested the boy to have his father secure the pistol after the Federals had left the town and return it to him. Just about a year after that Mr. Walker received the pistol. It had been brought back to Tennessee by the father of the boy, and after several transfers was safely returned to Mr. Walker.

Thomas Horatio McNish was associated with the Southern Methodist Publishing House for forty-four years and was a member of the Porter Rifles of which a short description will be given in the part of this history concerning Samuel Anderson McNish, brother of Thomas McNish.

Thomas Horatio McNish married, June 3, 1885, Emma Mann, born at Dixon Springs, Tennessee, December 23, 1861. The marriage ceremony was performed by the Reverend J. B. McFerrin, and the witnesses were Garnet N. Morgan, and Stirling P. Ferguson. Emma Mann was a daughter of Mitchell Perry and Sarah Ann (Stovall) Mann. A record from the office of the Adjutant general, in Washington, D. C., sets forth; "Mitchell Perry Mann, also borne as M. P. Mann, and not found as Mitchell Perry Mann, Private, Company D. Ninth (Ward's Regiment) Tennessee Cavalry." Mitchell Perry Mann served in the "Confederate Army, enlisted August 27, 1862, at Hartsville, also known as Dixon Springs, Tennessee, Union Prisoner of War. Was captured, July 19, 1863, near Buffington Island, Ohio, and imprisoned at Camp Douglas, Chicago, Illinois, where he died on October 4, 1864. The above named company served in General Morgan's command.

Children of Thomas Horatio and Emma (Mann) McNish:

i   Kate Allen McNish; born at Dixon Springs, Tennessee, June 2, 1886; married, May 8, 1907, William J. Allen, born June 15, 1884; son of James M. Allen, of Nashville, Tennessee.

ii David Kelly McNish; born July 30, 1890; married, first, November 21, 1912, Lucille Taylor; had one child, David Kelly McNish, Junior; born November 11, 1916; married, second, October 14, 1928, Betty Berry; have one daughter, Betty Katherine McNish, born August 1, 1929.

iii Thomas Horatio McNish; born October 5, 1894; member Company D, Twentieth Engineers, Forestry Division, in World War.

iv Emma Dean McNish; born April 3, 1898; died January 9, 1900.

v   Edgar McNish; born February 28, 1901.

Hugh Lawson McNish, son of William Dean and Julia Ann (Stump) McNish, was born April 25, 1857, and died May 23, 1918. He was named for Hugh Lawson White, one of the famous men of Tennessee, who was born in North Carolina, in 1773; became a prominent Judge in 1814; Senator in 1826, and, but for the bitter opposition of Andrew Jackson, it seems probable that he would have been elected Vice-President of the United States. Hugh Lawson McNish was also a member of the Porter Rifles with his brothers, Thomas, and Samuel, and referred to subsequently.

Hugh Lawson McNish married, December 31, 1884, Sarah Naomi (Bonnie) Green, a short sketch of whose family follows.

Thomas Green, ancestor of Sarah Naomi (Green) McNish, came to America on the "Speedwell." He had (perhaps others), Berryman Green, who later became known as Captain Berryman Green and was a member of Washington's Staff. His son, Thomas Jefferson Green, was born December 28, 1796, and married, at Chapel Hill, North Carolina, October 5, 1818, Frances Keeling Burton. She was born December 11, 1797, daughter of James Minge Burton, and his wife, Elizabeth Ridley, an account of whose family will follow.

James Ridley was the eldest son of Robert and Elizabeth A. Ridley, and was a native of Virginia. His son, Bromfield Ridley, was born in Southampton County, Virginia, and later removed to Oxford, Granville County, North Carolina, where he practiced law as early as 1770, and possibly earlier. Bromfield Ridley married Frances Henderson, daughter of Judge Henderson, whose wife was a Williams, a daughter of Judge Williams. The wife of Judge Williams was a daughter, it is said, of Lord George Keeling, whose property, it is also said, was lost in the troubles of the times.

Bromfield Ridley, son of James, acquired wealth and later owned a beautiful country-seat called "Nine Oaks," where he and his devoted wife, Frances Henderson, lived and raised a family of eight children, four sons and four daughters. He died in 1796 at the age of about sixty years. Their daughter, Elizabeth, as given above, married James Minge Burton.

Doctor John Burton Green, son of Thomas Jefferson Green, as mentioned before, was born in Halifax County, Virginia, September 10, 1820. He married, January 7, 1847, at the home of her father, James Walker, the ceremony being performed by the Right Reverend James H Otey, and the Right Reverend Leonidas Polk, Naomi Walker. Their children were Maria, Sara Naomi (Bonnie), Virginia, and one son, Walker.

A short history of Naomi Walker's family is given herewith.

James Walker settled in Columbia, Tennessee, at an early date. He was accompanied by an old Negro slave who had been with his family since Mr. Walker's birth. James Walker later became a merchant and, also, it is said, printed one of the first newspapers in Tennessee.

James Walker married Jane Knox Polk, a sister of President James Knox Polk, and daughter of Samuel Polk, of Iredell County, North Carolina, and his wife, Janet Knox. Janet Knox was a daughter of Captain James Knox, who was closely related to John Knox, the Covenanter and Reformer, of Scotland, whose fight against the Roman Catholic Church is mentioned in history. Janet Knox Polk was a member of the Presbyterian Church, devoted to her church, and gave the bell to the Columbia, Tennessee, Church when it was built. Captain James Knox married Lydia Gillespie, and four children, Jean or Jane, Naomi, Robert, and Thomas, are mentioned.

Samuel Polk, the father of Janet Knox Polk, came from a family which had served its country with patriotic zeal and which had profited from foresight and industry. He was a son of Colonel Ezekiel Polk, who, with several other members of the family, were important in the Mecklenburg Declaration of Independence and the events leading up to it.

About 1806, the Polks, Colonel Ezekiel, Major Samuel, and their families, emigrated to Tennessee and established themselves in the beautiful and fertile Maury County and immediately took an important part in the development of the country. Major Samuel Polk first lived about six miles from Columbia, at a place located on the present Franklin pike. He lived there until he built a large brick house on Seventh Street, in Columbia, Tennessee, now "The Polk Memorial Home." Besides attending to the developments of his extensive land holdings, Major Polk acted as surveyor, an occupation very important in the new undeveloped country. He is said to have been a quiet, unassuming, gentleman with a pleasant vein of humor, who made many friends, but never sought public office.

In the front yard of the old Ezekiel Polk homestead in Hardeman County, Tennessee, stands a mighty oak tree and at the base of this tree lies the remains of Colonel Ezekiel Polk, composer of what is probably one of the oddest epitaphs in the world. Having procured a slab and having the satisfaction of seeing that it was worded as he desired, it was placed in his carriage-house, there to remain until needed. After his funeral, which was carried out at he had instructed, the slab was put into place and many sightseers came to read the odd epitaph, the first verse being as follows:

"Here lies the dust of old E.P.,
One instance of Mortality,
Pennsylvania born, North Carolina bred,
He died in Tennessee upon his bed."

Colonel Ezekiel Polk came to Hardeman County about 1800 and settled one mile west of Bolivar, in North Carolina. His home, which was built in 1810, was similar in appearance to The Hermitage, the home of President Andrew Jackson.

Children of Hugh Lawson and Naomi (Green) McNish were:

i Jennie Roberta McNish; born October 10, 1885; married, April 27, 1911, William B. Hager; born February 5, 1885, son of Doctor and Mrs. P. H. Hager; had children: Patty Jane Hager, born November 24, 1913; died December 21, 1918; Bonnie McNish Hager; born August 17, 1917; Helen Isabella Hager born March 6, 1920; William Berry Hager; born April 16, 1922.

ii Hugh Lawson McNish, Junior; born April 7, 1887; married, May 27, 1920, Elizabeth Schell, who was born February 13, 1894; had one child, Jean McNish, born August 6, 1927.

iii John (Jack) Green McNish; born April 11, 1888; married, December 13, 1919, Ruth Deal, born in August, 1894.

iv Phillip McNish; born March 30, 1896; died September 13, 1926; served in World War in Battery D, 114th Field Artillery.

Samuel Anderson McNish, son of William Dean and Julia Ann (Stump) McNish, was born in Nashville, Tennessee, November 7, 1861, and died at Pine Bluff, Arkansas, December 1, 1930. He was buried at Lewisville, Arkansas.

Samuel McNish was a newspaper man a greater part of his life and wrote considerably under the name of "Peter Quince," his *nom-de-plume*. Following is a short poem composed shortly before his death.

"Its a mighty good world we live in —
I think its superb — fine,

>   Its the very best one I've met up with,
>   Since starting down the line.
> "I do not know from whence I came
>   Nor very much do I care,
> For when good things were handed out
>   I've certainly had my share.
> "When I bid farewell to this good old world,
>   And my barque puts out to sea,
> I'll say, Farewell, Farewell, Friend World,
>   You've certainly been good to me."

Samuel McNish was a member of the Porter Rifles and once won a silver cup given for the best drilled man. On one occasion his brother, Hugh Lawson McNish, a member of the same company, won a handsome medal which has been handed down to his son. The Porter Rifles was one of the first organizations of the South to revive interest in military spirit. It was organized in 1875 taking its name from James D. Porter, then Governor of the State of Tennessee, and later Chancellor of Peabody Normal College. They developed into a high class organization and in 1882, they carried off a large majority of contests in which they participated and were often banqueted—even in Memphis where their chief rivals, the Chickasaw Guards, were the favorites of the times. In 1877 they were highly complimented by even the Federal General, William T. Sherman.

The Porter Rifles won deserved recognition and were often ordered out by the Governor to be used as a guard or to suppress strikes. Their uniform first consisted of a red coat, yellow waistcoat, blue trousers, and a red cap.

The last public appearance of the Porter Rifles was when they gave an exhibition drill at the Tennessee Centennial, in 1897, after preparation for a month. Among the list of living members at that time were Thomas Horatio McNish and his brother, Samuel Anderson McNish.

Samuel Anderson McNish married, first, at Nashville, Tennessee, July 1, 1885, Annie Maria McFerrin who was born November 7, 1869, and died June 16, 1903. A short account of the McFerrin family follows.

William McFerrin, it is said, was a Revolutionary soldier of Scotch-Irish ancestry who had come to America in 1740 settling in York County, Pennsylvania. He had a son who became a preacher.

the Reverend James M. McFerrin, and who married Jane Campbell Berry. Their son, Doctor John Berry McFerrin, was born in Rutherford County, Tennessee, in 1807, and later was the author of a "History of Methodism in Tennessee."

James William McFerrin, son of the Reverend Doctor John Berry McFerrin, and father of Annie Maria McFerrin, mentioned above, was a member of the firm, Cook, Settle and Company, Boots and Shoes, Number Two, Public Square, Nashville, in 1873. James William McFerrin was married in Nashville and following is an account of an exciting adventure which occurred on the return from their wedding trip.

On the evening of their marriage they left for Louisville and Cincinnati where he had attended to some business,—later returning by boat. They boarded the steamer *United States* and about midnight it collided with the *America* and a great disaster followed. Both boats burned and many passengers perished either in the flames or were drowned in the Ohio River. In the *Republican Banner*, a newspaper of Nashville, under the date of December 8, 1868, were the details of the disaster as told by James William McFerrin.

"He says that he and his wife had hardly retired for the night when they received the compliment of a beautiful serenade from an Italian band. The sweet echoes of the music had scarcely died away before he was startled by the slight jar, which shook the vessel and caused the chandeliers to rattle. His wife suggested the possibility of an accident and feared something was the matter, but he quieted her fears by telling her it was merely the movement of the boat. He had but finished the sentence when alarming cries were heard in the cabin. He rushed into the hall from his stateroom which was number thirty-seven on the lower tier, Ladies Salon, and found it filled with smoke, with the fire blazing in front. Having quickly returned into the berth he hastily placed a life-preserver upon his wife and, dragging her after him, endeavored to make his way through the dense smoke and swaying, though bewildered, humanity, but both, momentarily suffocated and overpowered by another dense body of smoke, fell to the floor. His wife screamed out 'God save us' which aroused him, as his consciousness returned, being prostrated beneath the volume of smoke which rose to the roof. He caught her up, and again started forward, when a Negro porter warned him the other way, that the fire was coming from the direction in which he was going. He shoved the Negro aside and escaped with his precious burden through the pantry entrance at the side. Having reached the railing in front of the wheel-house next to the shore, he and his wife stepped over it so as to be in readiness to leap upon the *America*, which was gradually drifting nearer and nearer. It was a moment of suspense. It appeared to him that he stood there three minutes before the *America* came alongside during which time his wife desired to leap into the river rather than be burned, when he told her in an impressive tone,—to reassure her to be still that both could be saved if she would follow his directions. This appeared to give her confidence which she retained throughout the trying ordeal, in the most heroic manner, and implicity obeyed her husband's every direction.

"It was agreed that neither should survive the other, if they must perish, they would enter the watery grave with clasped hands. So soon as the *America* touched the *United States* he told her to jump, and they sprang at once upon the boiler deck of the *America* when that steamer struck the shore. Fears being entertained that the boilers of the ill-fated steamer would explode, they, with others, immediately regained the top of the bank. He requested her to look back upon the dreadful scene, which she refused to do, it being more than she could stand. They had escaped a horrible death, with such clothes as they could hastily gather, and suffered greatly from the cold. They walked and ran until they reached the house of a Mr. Jackson three-quarters of a mile from the shore. The night was raw and chilling and the ground wet from recent rains.

"On their arrival at the house fires were made by which they warmed themselves and dried their clothing. His wife was given a dress and himself furnished with a pair of stockings and ladies overshoes, in which he could only get his toes. His apparel up to this moment had consisted of his shirt and drawers, and a piece of a soldier's overcoat which he had picked up on his way from the boat. They remained at Mr. Jackson's house where they were most hospitably treated until next morning, when twelve or fifteen of the survivors were conveyed to Florence, where they were surrounded by an immense crowd. Here he procured an old coat and an ancient pair of pantaloons which he paid for with a gold ring, the only valuable he had managed to save except his lovely bride. The ring was returned, however, when the man from whom he purchaser the clothing became aware of the trials through which he had just passed. A friend having loaned him fifty cents he bought a hood for his bride. They soon after took passage on the *General*

Buel for Louisville, where they were received with many congratulations. They went to the Louisville Hotel where he was rejoined by Mr. Watson M. Cook, his father-in-law, who furnished them with everything they needed. Mr. McFerrin's loss by the disaster was fully twelve hundred dollars."

Samuel Anderson and Annie Maria (McFerrin) McNish were the parents of a daughter, Dora Cook McNish, who was born in Nashville, Tennessee, September 28, 1890, and married, January 22, 1911, John Poitesent Ferguson. They were married by the Reverend Phillips Care Fletcher in the Winfield Methodist Church at Little Rock, Arkansas. Their children were: John Wright Ferguson II, who was born at Little Rock, Arkansas, July 12, 1912, and James McFerrin Ferguson, born at Sweden, Arkansas, March 25, 1915.

The above mentioned Samuel Anderson McNish and his first wife, Annie Maria McFerrin, were also the parents of a daughter, Nellie Louise McNish, who died before birth, March 26, 1901, and who was buried at Lewisville, Arkansas.

Samuel Anderson McNish married, second, April 30, 1906, Grace Kirtly, who was born at LeGrande, Oregon, October 7, 1882. Her father married Susan Jane Miller, born in Missouri, January 21, 1857, and died December 24, 1831, daughter of Hiram and Martha (Roudon) Miller. Hiram Miller was in the Confederate Army and is buried at Little Rock, Arkansas. The paternal grandmother of Grace Kirtly was Pernila Sandford, of Kentucky. Samuel Anderson McNish and his second wife, Grace Kirtly, were the parents of one son, Samuel Dean McNish, born at New Lewisville, Arkansas, July 4, 1908.

In keeping with a custom of that time, after the death of Annie (McFerrin) McNish, cards announcing the funeral were sent to relatives and friends—as follows:

"The friends and acquaintances of the late Mrs. Annie M. McNish, Wife of S. A McNish, are respectfully requested to attend her funeral from the Methodist Episcopal Church 10:00 A. M. today, June 17th 1903. Conducted by Reverend A. M. Robertson. Interment at Wilson Cemetary at 11:00 A. M., New Lewisville, Arkansas, June 16, 1903."

Roberta Lee McNish, daughter of William Dean and Julia Ann (Stump) McNish, was born February 22, 1866, and died September 15, 1896. She attended Miss Sallie White's private school for young ladies, afterwards Dr. Price's school, which was located where the Vauxhall Apartment now stands.

Roberta Lee McNish married, June 4, 1885, Evan Shields Matthews, born January 27, 1862, son of Doctor Joseph Pillmore and Julia Ann (Shields) Matthews, Evan Shields Matthews was connected with the Southern Methodist Publishing House for forty years. A short outline of the Shields family,—the family of Evan Shields Matthews' mother—is given here.

John Jourdan Shields, was of Scotch-Irish descent and his father was a native of Virginia from whence several sons had left,—some moving west—while he removed to Hopkinsville, Kentucky, with Benjamin F. Shields, then his youngest son. Other children were born and reared in Kentucky. He enlisted in the Volunteer Service when quite young and was stationed at Norfolk, Virginia, during the War of 1812. He died October 9, 1871, receiving a pension for services to the United States up to the time of his death.

John Jourdan Shields married, in Harrodsburg, Kentucky, Mary Safferan, of German descent, and Virginian by birth. She is said to have been proud of her ancestry and a character that might have been envied by women of higher education. She was lofty in her sense of honor, and not only taught her children, but set an example which had an influence that lasted a lifetime. Her word was law and she was both loved and feared. She died June 19, 1859.

Records concerning her ancestry, or any data pertaining to her parentage, have not been found, but we know that she had brothers and sisters, John Safferan, Daniel Safferan, David Safferan, Mrs. —— Wood, Mrs. —— Weller, Malinda Safferan, and "Kitty" Safferan.

The children of Evan Shields and Roberta Lee (McNish) Matthews:

    i Julia Bessie Matthews; teacher in Nashville, Tennessee public schools.

    ii Nellie Matthews; born March 16, 1888, married September 17, 1907, Percy Cooper Cloyd, born February 27, 1886, son of Winfield Scott and Alice (Wilson) Cloyd; the former born October 10, 1845, and married Alice Wilson, December 28, 1884. Mrs. Alice Wilson Cloyd died November 11, 1935.

Percy Cloyd, Junior, son of Percy Cloyd and Nellie (Matthews) Cloyd was born March 17, 1910, and married March 23, 1935, Elizabeth Helen Hamilton.

Ellen Rae Cloyd, daughter of Percy C. Cloyd, Junior, was born July 28, 1937.

iii Evan Shields Matthews, Junior; born May 27, 1892; married Viola Betz; children, Ruth, Dorothy and Betty.

iv Robert Gilbert Matthews; born in August 1895; died November 21, 1895.

Evan Shields Matthews married, second time, June 8, 1898, Nellie Wharton Wilson, and their children were: John Hunter Matthews, born April 9, 1901.

Martha Dake Matthews (called Dot), born May 23, 1903; married Frank Gilliam, November 26, 1924.

James William McFerrin married, December 1, 1868, Dora Cooke, a short account of whose family follows.

Major Richard F. Cooke was an officer under General Andrew Jackson, during the War of 1812, and was several times elected to the Senate of Tennessee. His son, the Honorable Richard F. Cooke, who resided near Edgefield, at that time one of the beautiful environs of Nashville, was the father of Colonel Watson M. and Bolivar H. Cooke. The latter, Bolivar H. Cooke, owned, in 1867, a wholesale clothing house called Bolivar H. Cooke and Company.

Colonel Watson M. Cooke, father of Dora Cooke, mentioned above, was born in Jackson County, Tennessee, in September, 1817. After a liberal education there, and later in college, he went to Gainsboro, in the spring of 1837, and started the firm of Cooke, Bailey and Company, shoe merchants, until the breaking out of the war. He found that he could hope to do little business under the prevailing permit system, so he, in company with Hugh Douglas and Colonel William Webb, went to Louisville, in 1863, continuing there until 1865 when he became a member of the wholesale boot and shoe firm, Cooke, Settle and Company, where he remained until his death. His church affiliations were with the Tulip Street Church where he served as a steward.

Colonel Watson M. Cooke married, in Gainsboro, Tennessee, Maria Ann Shores, of Virginia, a niece of Colonel Bransford. She was a true daughter of the "Old South," having been born in Virginia, in 1814. She was gracious, hospitable, cultured, and dignified, as became the daughters of the period just prior to the war who were given much to entertaining. She died in St. Louis, in her eighty-ninth year at the home of her daughter, Mrs. E. S. Lewis.

Nellie Louise McNish, youngest child of William Dean and Julia Ann (Stump) McNish, was born March 18, 1875. She married William Wheless Gambill. An account of their children and grandchildren, as well as a history of the Gambill family has been given in Part I. As shown in the said Part I of the present work, William Wheless Gambill was a descendant of Captain James Leeper and Susan Drake, his wife.

Dean

[1] THE REVEREND WILLIAM DEAN was born probably in Ireland about 1719 and came to America before 1742 as it is known that in this year he was licensed by the Presbytery of New Brunswick, New Jersey, and officiated at various times in New Jersey, Pennsylvania and Virginia. His license was dated August 12, 1742, and he was soon sent to Neshaminy and the Forks of the Delaware. In 1745 he went into Virginia, but the following year he was ordained pastor of the congregation at the Forks of the Brandywine, in Pennsylvania. He died July 9, 1748 at the early age of twenty-nine years after several years of active, zealous and faithful ministry.

The Reverend William Dean married and became the father of the following children:

    i   Benjamin Dean; probably a merchant in Philadelphia and mentioned in a court record of his brother, William Dean.

    ii   A daughter, probably Sarah, wife of the Reverend John Slemmons, of Marsh Creek, York County, Pennsylvania, mentioned in court record of her brother, William Dean.

[2]iii   Joseph Dean; of whom subsequently.

    iv   John Dean; a Major during the Revolutionary War; mentioned in court record of his brother, William Dean.

    v   William Dean; a Colonel during the Revolutionary War; did valiant duty at Princeton, Trenton, and Germantown; owned two hundred sixty-five acres of land in Augusta County, Virginia, later devised to his brothers and sister.

[2]Joseph Dean, son of the Reverend William Dean, was born August 10, 1738 at Ballymenagh, County of Antrim, Ireland. He apparently came to America with his father and later became an important importing merchant in Philadelphia. During this time he was a signer of the celebrated Non-importation resolutions which was an agreement made by merchants in this country not to import from England certain enumerated articles in retaliation for the high excise duty which was being imposed on us by England.

Some of the more important positions held by Joseph Dean were: Member of the Committee of the City, 1774; Delegate to the Provincial Congress, 1775; Member of the Committee of Safety, 1776;

JOSEPH DEAN
*Copy of portrait which hangs in the Historical
Society Library in Philadelphia*

Member of the Board of War, 1777; and Warden of the Port, in 1781. His portrait was painted by Charles Wilson Peale and hangs on the second floor in the Historical Society of Pennsylvania building.

Joseph Dean had an excellent War service during the Revolution. He enlisted April 27, 1777 as a private in Captain George Stoughton's Company and, about December, 1777, was transferred to Kirkpatrick's Company, same Regiment. In April, 1778, he was transferred to Captain Stoughton's Company and in June, the same year, he was transferred to Captain Kirkpatrick's Company. He was transferred later in 1778 to different companies, and finally, in December, 1779, was mustered out. He died September 9, 1793.

Joseph Dean married, first, Frances McCracken, who died March 1, 1793, and second, Hannah Boyd, who died June 28, 1823. Their remains lie interred in the Moravian Cemetery at the corner of Franklin and Vine Streets, in Philadelphia.

Joseph and Hannah (Boyd) Dean were the parents of a daughter:
[3]i Susan Dean; of whom subsequently.

[3]Susan Dean, daughter of Joseph and Hannah (Boyd) Dean, was born April 25, 1800, and died January 6, 1875. She married Horatio McNish and further account of this family will be found under the history of the McNish family.

Stump

COLONEL FREDERICK STUMP was born in Heidelburg Township, Pennsylvania, in 1723, and died in May, 1822. During the winter of 1802-1803, he commanded a company under Colonel George Doherty and traveled as far as Natchez to assist in taking possession of Louisiana. He had made his head-quarters there by invitation of Governor Claiborne, an old friend, and was present when Sutton and May came to claim a one thousand dollar reward which had been offered to any who would bring the head of a certain outlaw named Mason to Governor Claiborne. The Governor told them to call at a certain time and a check should be ready for them. Colonel Stump was present at this meeting, and after they had gone, said he believed that Sutton was really "Little" Harpe, a well-known outlaw, as was his brother, or father, known as "Big" Harpe. Colonel Stump offered a reward for the apprehension of the Harpes and as Sutton had answered the description of "Little" Harpe, both men who had come and claimed the reward above were arrested. Some interested person had said that "if he is Harpe, he had a mole on his neck, and two toes grown together on one foot." This proved to be true on the person of the so-called Sutton, and the fellow, with such positive proof against him, shed tears.

Another story about Colonel Stump concerns his leaving for Georgia. A party of eleven Shawanees came to his house while intoxicated with the intention of killing Colonel Stump. It was a bright moon-light night and upon reaching the house they began cutting down the door and through the opening they made crept in, one by one. They were met, on the threshold, however, by the resolute Colonel, who, with an old meat-axe, cut them down as fast as they entered, until he had killed nine of them—the other two escaping. The Colonel then went in pursuit of them, found their camp, and stole up and tomahawked them. This act was investigated by the Quakers and the Colonel was imprisoned. He was released, however, by a group of men known as the "Paxton Boys," who had, at one time, caused a great sensation by murdering nearly a whole tribe of Indians without punishment from the Government. Colonel Stump fled to Georgia, settled there, and acquired property and standing.

Colonel Stump had served during the Revolutionary War and during a fight near Augusta, under Colonel Marion, had continued fighting after the Americans had chiefly retreated—was finally overpowered and taken prisioner. He claimed to have killed five British officers and was sent to St. Augustine where he was confined four months, but finally bribed the jailor for ten guineas and escaped without discovery. The news of his escape reached Georgia before him—a reward was offered by the British for him, dead or alive, and, because his grist and saw mills had been burned, his twenty negroes taken, he was reduced to poverty. He then decided to "go West" and finally, somewhere in the eastern part of Tennessee, fell in with Amos Eaton, Haydon Wells, Benjamin and John Drake, Isaac Rounsevell, Thomas Ramsey and others, passed through the Kentucky wilderness, and on the 24th of December, 1779, made a halt at the ford of White Creek, four miles northwest of the now City of Nashville, and a mile from the Cumberland River. Here they pitched their tents, remaining until Spring, when they chose individual locations, each settling on their chosen spot. They raised crops for two seasons without molestation from the Indians, but soon after there began a series of combats which ended in a massacre on a creek, ever since known as Battle Creek. But one person escaped this massacre, Mrs. Sarah Berry, who, later, met by Colonel Stump, was carried, with her child, to safety to Eaton's. She subsequently married Shadrack Jones, and her little child grew to womanhood, married, and became the mother of several children.

The early records of Davidson County, Tennessee, have record of Frederick Stump, and his son, Frederick, Junior, as tax payers in 1780 and the Tennessee records of the War of 1812 show that Frederick, Junior, as Captain Frederick Stump, served under Colonel John Coffee in the Volunteer Cavalry, enlisting December 10, 1812, for twelve months service "for the defense of the lower country." He enlisted again on September 24, 1813 with service under John Alcorn until December 10, 1813.

From a report of the journey of Brethern Abraham Steiner and Frederick G. D. Schev to the Cherokees and the Cumberland settlements, we learn that they "crossed the Cumberland on a ferry, here shut in by steep rock. Several miles from the river is Frederick Stump's plantation, fine and large, along White Creek. Through this runs the road that leads from Nashville to Clarksville. He conducts an inn, has a mill and fourteen other plantations by which he has rented to people at the rate of fifteen bushels of corn for every acre that is cultivated."

From land records in North Carolina we find the following: "Know Ye that we have granted unto Frederick Stump 640 acres of land in Davidson County lying on White's Creek. Beginning at a hickory in David Rounseval's line with the same South forty-five West one hundred and fifty-six poles to a sugar tree and ash, corner to David Rouseval's, thence West one hundred and ten poles to a stake, north four hundred fifty-two poles to an ash, East crossing the creek two hundred and fifty-one poles to a black walnut; West, crossing the Creek thirty-seven poles to the beginning. To hold unto the said Frederick Stump, his heirs and assign forever.
Dated 17th of April, 1786. (Book G, Page 36.)

R. C. Caswell.

I. Glasgow, Sec'y.
Warrant No. 139: James Saunders, D. S.
James Flack. James Hamilton, C. C."

After the death of Colonel Frederick Stump, the division of the negroes and Chattels of his estate was returned into Court and acknowledged by Philip Shute and John Criddle, two of his Executors, to be their act and ordered to be recorded. This was recorded December 27, 1826, in Book 9, Page 67, of Davidson County Court, October Sessions, State of Tennessee, and follows:

"Agreeable to the last will and testament of Frederick Stump, deceased, we, the undersigned Executors, should proceed in the forepart of the Year, 1822, to divide the estate between the families of John Stump and Christopher Stump, sons of Frederick, after paying over to Barbara Cox, a daughter of said Frederick, a legacy left her of two negroes. We proceed and divided in the following manner, viz: We alloted and set apart to John Stump's family, negroes, Alcey and two children, Tony, Class, Nelson, William, Phillis, Jude, Daniel, Tom, Nell, Dick, Charles, Nathan, Jack Easter, Cloe, Ben, Vine, Jack, Henry, Silphey, Edmond, Ishmail, Shade, Matilda, Fanny, Abram, and Lewis, in all thirty in number. We allotted and set apart to Christopher Stump's family negroes; old Winney Jinney and her children; Peter, Manuel, Mary and her three children, Bill, Little Tony, Isaac, Letty, Lovy, Anthony, Winny, Nancy, Stephen, Lucy, Caty, George, Loser, Sam, Peter, Washington, Betty, Licer, and Abt, also thirty in number. The perishable property we set up and sold for the purpose of making a division between the two families, the money equal admitting John Stump to bid for such as he thought the most necessary for his family and he bid off six ploughs, one lot of ploughs, hoes, two hoes and scythe, one shelling machine, four axes, three hoes, one wheat fan, five bedsteads and furniture, one white mare, one gray horse, one iron gray mare, one sorrell horse, one bay, one bay, one bay, one bay, one wagon, one grindstone, three cows and calves, one yellow cow, one red cow and calf, one red cow, one red cow, one dun cow and yearling, one red cow, twenty sheep, one cupboard, one table, twelve chairs which we set apart to his family at the price's bid off at amounting to $568.52. The balance we set apart to Christopher Stump's family amounting to $549.40, the whole having been laid off or sold for the sum of eleven hundred and seventeen dollars and ninety-two cents including all stock, household and kitchen furniture, and all articles sold at the sale of the perishable property of said Frederick Stump, deceased, by said Executors. Witness our hands and seals this 27th day of June, 1826.

      Philip Shute
      John Criddle
      Thomas Shute."

A Will of Colonel Frederick Stump was dated March 26, 1820, and recorded in Book of Wills and Inventories, Volume 7, pages 501 to 505. This will was offered for probate, but was contested by heirs, in as much as a Will made on a prior date, November 25, 1819, took precedence over the former one. This was just prior to the record showing the division of his estate in 1826. The Will of 1819 was probated and the property divided as per its terms, and was divided as follows:—to Catherine Stump, his widow in free simple, three hundred acres, and his home place on White's Creek; to Rachel Stump, two hundred and thirty-seven acres; to Thomas Jefferson Stump, two hundred nine acres; to John F. Stump, two hundred fourteen acres; to Phil Stump, two hundred thirty-four acres, and to Tennessee Stump, two hundred thirty-four acres.

Colonel Frederick Stump married, first, Ann Snevly, and second, May 6, 1816, when he was ninety-three years of age, to Catherine Gingry. She was about twenty-five years of age when married, and lived to be an old lady.

The children of Colonel Frederick Stump follow, but the order of their birth is not known:

  i Jacob Stump; of whom subsequently.
  ii Barbara Stump; married —— Cox.

iii Colonel John Stump; born in October, 1776; mentioned in records with father.
iv A daughter; married Jonathan Gais.
v Christopher Stump; of whom subsequently.
vi Frederick Stump, Junior; born in 1783; resided on Big Barren, fourteen miles below Bowling Green, Kentucky; killed by Indians when he was twenty-two years of age; married, and father of three children.

Jacob Stump, son of Colonel Frederick Stump, with his brother-in-law, Jonathan Gais, went one morning in search of Indians, followed their trail up Wells' Creek where they soon found moccasin tracks, and in a few minutes discovered four Indians sitting on a log picking their flints. They had not seen the white man who had arranged that Stump fire first and Gais reserve his shot for emergency. Jacob Stump fired so that he killed two of the Indians with one shot, then, both the white men fled for the fort. They were intercepted, however, by another party of Indians and this time Jacob Stump was shot and killed. Putman's History of Tennessee states that "when the Indians killed Jacob Stump, and gave chase to 'Old man Frederick,' it was a close race for three miles to Eaton's—up hill and down dale, through cane and into cedars near the station, where it was stoop here, shy there, fleeing from pursuers. They were very close upon him several times—so near as to strike at him with their hatchets, which one of them finally threw with such violence and accuracy that, passing near his head with a whiz, it fell in the bushes twenty feet before him. He supposed the Indian stopped to hunt for it and followed no further. He used to say, 'Py sure, I tid run dat time.' "

Christopher Stump, son of Colonel Frederick Stump, was born in 1778, and died July 12, 1821. He was a Captain of Troop Number 4, Tennessee Cavalry, in the Natchez Expedition. This expedition went from Tennessee and neighboring states to Alabama subsequent to the terrible massacre of Americans by the Creek Indians, and was commanded by General Coffee. Colonel Stump was an Alderman in Nashville in 1818.

Christopher Stump married, first, Sarah Brooks, who died in 1807, and second, August 3, 1811, Rachel Shute.

Christopher and Sarah (Brooks) Stump were the parents of Thomas Jefferson Stump, of whom more will be given subsequently, and there may have been other children although no record has been found.

Thomas Jefferson Stump, son of Christopher and Sarah (Brooks) Stump, was born July 12, 1804, and died in California, in May, 1852. In 1849, during the Gold Rush, in company with his two sons, he started for California to seek gold. From Thompson's "History of the People of the United States," we find the following reference to the gold rush. "Early in 1848 shining particles of yellow metal were found on the land of John A. Sutter near the present city of Sacramento. News spread over the United States and by 1849 there began a rush to the gold fields. All through the spring and summer so many thousands went that they formed an almost unbroken train from the outskirts of Missouri to the foot of the Rocky Mountains. Sacramento, a settlement probably of not more than two hundred inhabitants in April, became a thriving city of nearly two thousand by October. 'Forty-niners' were mostly Americans. As there were no laws for the territory, a condition bordering on anarchy prevailed. The better element, considering it imprudent to wait for Congress to provide a Government for the wild country, adopted a Constitution in November, 1849."

Also from an old newspaper clipping, in 1932, it is noted that a revival of the scene, eighty-three years before, took place, after the finding of a huge nugget valued at one thousand and twenty dollars.

Thomas Jefferson Stump often used to write poetry and one of his poems has come down to us from his sister, Julia Stump McNish, who quoted it from memory, in 1916, at the age of eighty-two. It is as follows:

> "I am to cross the desert wide,
> To find the precious treasure;
> To settle by the Ocean's tide
> And dig when I'm at leisure.
> A sister I at home will leave;
> A brother 'till he is older.
> If there's no other way to go
> I'll enter as a soldier.
> A father I will have to guide me,
> As I travel through by land,
> And the host of friends I'll have beside me
> Will form our little band.

Nothing more have I to say,
Only may good luck attend you;
And should you ever come to Monterey
With our laws will we defend you."

Thomas Jefferson Stump married, December 21, 1825, Melinda Tennessee Marshall, daughter of Elihu Marshall. A short sketch of the Marshall family follows subsequently herein

The children of Thomas Jefferson and Melinda Tennessee (Marshall) Stump follow:

i   Frederick C. Stump; born Sunday, October 1, 1826, died in 1888; married Lena ——; had children: Emma Stump; Julia Stump; Mollie Stump; Cornelia Stump, and Thomas Stump.

ii   George W. Stump; born Sunday, November 2, 1828.

iii   Thomas Jefferson Stump, Junior; born April 24, 1831; died August 13, 1881; married, September 11, 1856, Novella Frazier, of California had children: Freddy Stump; born June 26, 1857; Julia Frances Stump; born September 2, 1839, in California; married —— Troup; Belle Stump; married —— Crosby, of California.

iv   Julia Ann Stump; of whom subsequently.

v   John T. Stump; born Sunday, March 12, 1837; died in California, unmarried.

vi   Melinda Tennessee Stump; born November 23, 1839; died September 16, 1841.

vii   Albert Henry Stump; died in 1843.

viii   William Harvey Stump; died in June, 1844, an infant.

Julia Ann Stump, daughter of Thomas Jefferson and Melinda Tennessee (Marshall) Stump, was born March 8, 1834, and died January 19, 1919. Her mother died when she was but ten years of age and she went to live with her Aunt, Katherine (Marshall) Brown. It is said they were very kind to her and never in any way showed any preference between her and their own children.

She attended the old Nashville Female Academy of which her grandfather, Christopher Stump, and her great-uncle, John Stump, were among the original stock-holders. Her father, Thomas Jefferson Stump, was at one time one of its Trustees. This Academy was chartered in 1816 and ceased to exist in 1860. From Clayton's "History of Davidson County, Tennessee," we learn that "greatly to the honor of Nashville . . . her citizens were the first in the United States appreciating the separateness and the importance of female education enough to demand an institution chartered for that purpose (the higher education of women), and it is to the credit of the gentlemen organizing the Academy that they used their money and influence at that early day thus to dignify female education. . . . . ." It was the rich man's school and its patronage was known to be the largest. It was also known to be the richest in the United States. It was located on Church Street at Ninth Avenue, and was under the direction of the Reverend Doctor C. D. Elliott. During the Civil War, the building was used as a barracks by the Fifty-first Regiment of Ohio Volunteers. Again quoting from the history of Davidson County, "the pupils of the Academy lived in an atmosphere of honor. All letters to them by mail were delivered into their own hands, and they, by mail, could send letters to whom they pleased. Correspondence was sacred."

A programme printed on white satin was treasured by Julia Ann Stump, later in life after her marriage, as a souvenir of the occasion when she was a bride and went to hear the famous Swedish nightingale, Jenny Lind, on the occasion of her concert in Nashville. This program was destroyed along with other things valued for their age and associations when the home of Julia Ann Stump McNish, at 603 Woodland Street, East Nashville, was destroyed by fire, March 22, 1916. On March 8th she had celebrated her eighty-second birthday with a like number of candles on her birthday cake, receiving a great number of cards and presents and a poem written for her by her brother-in-law. An account of the first, given sixteen years afterward, is as follows: "Sixteen years ago Nashville had its greatest fire. Nine hundred and seventy-eight buildings, including structures of all types, were reduced to ashes in East Nashville of the city. Block after block was swept away. Fanned by a high wind, flames and cinders jumped to propogate anew several houses away. Firemen, with aid from practically every city surrounding, battled away five hours before the flames were under control. The ruins smouldered for two days. The first alarm was sounded at 11:49 A. M. First firemen to arrive saw the quickness with which the flames spread and called for help. Help came, and then more help. Every piece of apparatus in the city was in use. By early afternoon the press of a nation was watching a city battle to retain what it had erected. Charge after charge of dynamite was set off in a futile attempt to stop the blazing advance. Tricks of fate, where furniture was moved into the street and destroyed while the house was saved, fringed with disaster. Relief measures for the homeless began immediately. Damage estimated by the fire department at more than one million, five hundred thousand dollars, had been done in a day. Ruin extended from the starting point at 214 North First Street to 808 Dews, in Southeast Nashville." News of the fire soon spread over the country and Julia Ann Stump McNish received numerous telegrams as to her safety.

Julia Ann Stump married William Dean McNish and the continuation of this family will be found under the history of the McNish family.

Marshall

ELIHU MARSHALL lived in Nashville, Tennessee, at the time of his death which was some time after March 7, 1829, the date of his will. This will, recorded in Book 9, page 351, of Davidson County, Tennessee, records, is as follows:

"In the name of God, Amen, I, Elihu Marshall of Nashville, in the county of Davidson and state of Tennessee, being weak in body, but of sound and perfect mind and memory, do make and publish this my last will and Testament in manner and form following:— that is to say, I give and bequeath to my beloved wife, Elizabeth Marshall, to have and to hold for an during the terms of her natural life all my real and personal property, including my brick house and lot on Market Street in Nashville where I now reside, also one female slave named Rachel together with all the rest residue and remainder of my property, goods and chattels of what kind soever and my will and desire is that at the death of my wife all the property so given and bequeathed shall be divided equally between our children should the youngest be at that time twenty-one years of age, but if the youngest child shall not have arrived at the age of twenty-one years at the death of my wife, then and in case the property is to remain undivided until the youngest child shall have attained the age of twenty-one years when it shall be divided as above specified, and I do appoint my wife Elizabeth sole Executor of my last well anl testament revoking hereby all other former wills by me made. In Testamony whereof I have hereunto set my hand and seal at Nashville this March 7th 1829.

Elihu Marshall

"State of Tennessee, Davidson County, October Sessions, 1829. A paper writing purporting to be the last will and Testament of Elihu Marshall deceased was produced in open court for probate and proved thus; William H. Barker, Addison East, and Eben H. Burnett, the subscribing witnesses to the paper being duly sworn, depose and say that they became such in the presence of the deceased Elihu and at his request and they verily believe he was of sound deposing mind and memory at the time of executing the deceased paper. It is therefore ordered by the court that deceased paper be admitted to record as such will of Elihu Marshall."

The inventory of the estate of Elihu Marshall, deceased, was recorded September 3, 1830 and is as follows:

"Inventory of the estate of Elihu Marshall, deceased. One negro woman, Rachel about forty years of age, five bedsteads and furniture, one clock, large kind, one pair of mahogany# dining table, three common tables, three dozen chairs, one common settee, one cupboard, two presses, one pair looking glasses, pair shovel and tongs, five iron pots and kettles, two pair sad irons, three pair fire dogs, one pair waffle irons, one old turkey carpet, one common carpet, three dozen silver spoons, table and teaspoons, three dozen knives and forks, two sets china cups and saucers, two brass kettles, seven trunks, a few dozen band-boxes. An inventory of the estate of Elihu Marshall deceased was returned into court on oath by Elizabeth Marshall his Executrix and order to be recorded.

Testator, Henry Ewing, Clerk of said Court."

Elihu Marshall married Elizabeth Smith who died July 7, 1839, daughter of Peter Smith.

Elihu and Elizabeth (Smith) Marshall had the following children, although perhaps there were others:

 i Melinda Tennessee Marshall, described subsequently.
 ii A son described subsequently.
 iii Katherine (Kitty) Marshall; described subsequently.

Melinda Tennessee Marshall, daughter of Elihu and Elizabeth (Smith) Marshall, was born October 8, 1808, and died April 14, 1844. She attended the old Nashville Female Academy and later married Thomas Jefferson Stump. A further account of their children is given under the history of the Stump family.

Katherine (Kitty) Marshall married Berry H. Brown. They were the parents of the following children:

 i John T. (Tobe) Brown; born October 23, 1828; died September 18, 1905; married Addie Payne, who died July 31, 1881; children: Lillie M. Brown, died March 11, 1904; Lucian Massey Brown; born April 3, 1859; died July 20, 1864.
 ii Ash Brown; remained unmarried.
 iii Richard Brown; member of original Ku Klux; removed to Texas where he died unmarried.

 #Worded thus, in the copy of this Inventory furnished for use of the compiler of these records.

- iv Polk Brown; married Sallie Brown, a member of the Sumner County, Tennessee, family and relationship, if any, not known.
- v Mollie Brown; born in 1837; died in 1898: married —— Cockrill had one son.
- vi Ella Brown; died January 2, 1893; married William Quinton Smith; described further subsequently.

Elihu and Elizabeth (Smith) Marshall most certainly had a son whose name has not come down to us as his, the son's, daughter, Martha, was known to be a cousin to Julia Ann Stump, daughter of Thomas Jefferson Stump and his wife Melinda Tennessee Marshall, daughter of Elihu. This son was married three times and had the following children by his first wife:

- i Elihu, called "Lydy" settled and died in Weatherford, Texas.
- ii Benjamin Marshall; died a few years after the Civil War.
- iii Charles Marshall; died in Chicago, Illinois.
- iv Henry W. (or William H.) Marshall; member of Company G, 18th Tennessee Infantry; resided at one time at Union City, Tennessee; died at Confederate Soldier's Home, near The Hermitage.
- v Martha Marshall; described subsequently.

Martha Marshall, grand-daughter of Elihu and Elizabeth (Smith) Marshall, had two step-mothers, but went to live later with her cousin, Julia Stump McNish. She married, first, in 1865, Captain James C. Thomas, son of Ennis and Amanda Thomas, of Covington, Kentucky, who had six sons in the Civil War,—three in the Union Army and three in the Confederate Army. He, himself, was a Captain in the Union Army and met his future wife when "the Yankees took Nashville," and married her just after Lee's surrender.

Martha Marshall had children only by her first husband, Captain James Thomas, and were as follows:

- i Will Thomas; unmarried; employed by City of Chicago, Illinois for about forty years.
- ii Flora Thomas; married Beckham Lee Douglas, of Texas; have children:
  - 1 William (Billy) Douglas; married Marguerite Cummings, of Durango, Colorado; graduate of

University of Colorado; have child, Sallie Sue Douglas.

2 Katheryn Virginia Douglas; married Thomas Henry Busey on November 29, 1930, at St Barnabas Church, Denver, Colorado; the Buseys having been pioneers from Virginia to Texas—later to Colorado.

Ella Brown, daughter of Berry H. Brown and his wife, Katherine Marshall, died January 2, 1893. As stated above she married William Quinton Smith, a prominent lawyer of Nashville at the time of his marriage. They removed to Alabama, near Montgomery, where their home, "Violet Hill," was considered one of the handsomest in Alabama. William Quinton Smith died in 1912. James Quinton Smith, a nephew of William Quinton Smith, was formerly Attorney-General for the State of Alabama, and married Erline Crittenden. They are the parents of a daughter, Marie Smith. James Quinton Smith, Senior, father of James Quinton Smith, married Marie Fair, daughter of General E. Y. Fair, of Montgomery, Alabama, who at one time represented the United States in Belgium. The name Quinton has come down in the Smith family from generation to generation, dating back to England from where the Smiths originally came.

William Quinton and Ella (Brown) Smith were the parents of the following children:

i Maggie Lee Smith; born August 24, 1868; married Andrew Jackson Briggs, who was born in 1864 and died in September, 1900, a Methodist Minister; had children:

1 Andrew Jackson Briggs, Junior; married Ethel Rogge, of Dayton, Ohio.

2 Ella Brown Briggs; married Dorster Laney, member of well-known Laney family of Alabama; children: Mary Louise Laney and Margaret Laney.

ii Armatine Quinton Smith; born December 24, 1871; married, April 18, 1893, Green McKinney Featherstone, born January 11, 1863; died December 25, 1927; member of Order of Red Men; Past Grand Sachem for State of Alabama member of Methodist Church; associated with Braid Electric Company, Nashville, Tennessee;

son of Henry Daniel Featherstone who died in September, 1907 and his wife, Margaret Bell, who died November 20, 1898.

iii Mary Louise Smith; born in 1879; married Thomas Paten Banks; reside Charlotte, North Carolina; have children: Richard Thomas Banks, who married, April 15, 1932, Edith Sue Harris, born September 11, 1911; daughter of James Benjamin Harris, born October 29, 1852, died July 2, 1926, and his wife, Mary Sue Jones, born July 16, 1875; married James Benjamin Harris, December 16, 1891; and II Edwin McKinney Banks, born May 14, 1912.

Part III
TENNESSEE HISTORICAL MISCELLANY

Tennessee As It Was Soon After the Marriage of Captain James Leeper and Susan Drake

(From *The American Pocket Atlas* Published
in 1796 by Matthew Carey, Philadelphia

"THIS STATE is divided into eleven counties: Washington, Green, Hawkins, Knox, Jefferson, Sevier, Blount, Davidson, Sumner and Tennessee.

"The Cumberland Mountain, in its whole extent from the Great Kanawha to the Tennessee consists of the most stupendous piles of craggy rocks of any mountain in the Western Country. 'The Whirl,' as it is called, is compared to the width of about one hundred yards. Just as it enters the mountains a large rock projects from the northern shore in an oblique direction, which renders the bed of the river still narrower and causes a sudden bend; the water of the river is, of course, thrown with great rapidity against the southern shore, whence it rebounds around the point of rocks and produces the whirl, which is about eighty yards in circumference. In less than a mile below the whirl the river spreads into common width, and, except at the Muscle Shoals, is beautiful and smooth till it mingles with the Ohio.

"The Cumberland, or Great Laurel Ridge, is the most stupendous pile in the United States. It abounds with ginseng and stone coal. Clinch Mountain is south of these, in which Burk's Garden and Morris Knob might be described as curiosities.

"A few years since this country abounded with large herds of wild cattle, improperly called buffaloes; they are still to be found in some of the south branches of Cumberland River. Enough of bears and wolves yet remain. Beavers and others are caught in plenty in the upper branches of Cumberland and Kentucky Rivers; the mommoth, the king of the land animals, was supposed formerly an inhabitant of this country.

"The Presbyterians are the prevailing denomination of Christians in this district. There are also some of the Baptist and Methodist denominations.

"Three colleges are established by law in this state, Greenville College in Greene County, Blount College at Knoxville and Washington College in Washington county. A society has been established who style themselves 'A Society for Promoting Useful Knowledge.'

"Knoxville, beautifully located on the Holston, is the seat of government. At Nashville, the courts for the Districts of Mero are semi-annually held, and it has two houses for public worship, and a handsomely endowed academy.

"The Indian tribes are the Cherokees and the Chickasaws. The Cherokees have been a warlike and numerous nation, but by continual wars in which it has been their destiny to be engaged with the Northern Indians, they are reduced and have become weak and pusillanimous. The Chickasaws merit the most from Americans, having at all times maintained a brotherly attachment to them. They are a personable people, and have an openness in their countenance and behavior, uncommon among savages. These nations say they are the remnant of a great nation that once lived far to the west, which was destroyed by the Spaniards from whom they still retain a hereditary hatred.

"Tennessee was the sixteenth state taken into the Union and was admitted June 1, 1796."

THE PIONEERS OF TENNESSEE
Description by J. W. M. Breazeale, in 'Life As It Is," a Book Published in 1842 by James Williams

"If the fashionable and indolent portion of the citizens of Tennessee at the present day were compelled to resort to the same means for sustenance, which were used by their territorial ancestors, they would, no doubt expect soon to be plunged into a state of starvation, famine, and death. But our hardy and enterprising fathers lived comfortably, and contributed to bring out of their mother earth, a plentiful supply of all necessary vegetables to satisfy the cravings of hunger, and the indispensable wants of nature. They had the whole county before them; settled upon the most fertile spots; and cultivated them long before they were disturbed by the speculator and land jobber. They lived in harmony, friendship and brotherly love with each other. Generous hospitality and kindness reigned over the land, and if a stranger came amongst them he was received with open arms, treated to a rich feast of fat bear's meat and venison, and regaled with floods of milk and honey; for after the lapse of a few years the inhabitants had raised herds of cattle, and the forest was literally a vast store-house of the rich, delicious production of the industrious and busy bee.

"When a stranger who visited the settlers in these then newly populated regions departed he had no bill to pay, but carried with him the good wishes and pious benediction of his generous host; and, if a new emigrant came and settled in the country, he was immediately supplied with every necessary of life which his wants demanded, so far as the inhabitants possessed the means of ministering to his comfort and convenience.

"Peace, independence, and freedom pervaded the whole country. The inhabitants had not the expenses of an extravagant and prodigal government to bear, and, although apparently poor in this world's goods, they had at their command exhaustless stores of wealth, for all the flocks and herds of the forest were theirs. Their waterfowl lived in a hundred lakes and rivers. Their deer drank at five hundred streams, and their buffalo bounded over a thousand hills.

"Such were the first inhabitants of Tennessee, and such their character, habits, and conditions. But, as days and years rolled by, a change came over the spirit of the times and transformed the fashions, habits, and pursuits of the inhabitants. For several years the citizens of this new colony lived without any government, except that which they established for themselves. They had travelled into the country through the forest where no trace of the foot of civilized man could be seen. They brought hither their little household goods upon the backs of their horses and cattle and consequently there was not a wagon or other wheel carriage in all the country."

The Cumberland Compact

On May 1, 1780, the Cumberland Compact was signed by about two hundred and fifty pioneers, who had made settlement in the valley of the Cumberland River. These valiant fighters against the savage wilderness and savage men, far behind the civilization of the communities from which they had come, resolved to form a new American community, bulwarked by law and order. The greatness of America resulted from such ideals and resolves and deeds, by men who, like those founders of Tennessee, had courage to fight, grit to endure, and who cherished liberty and were determined that it should be the heritage, as it is the right, of every American.

The Signers of the Cumberland Compact set forth therein their sense of its necessity, and gave their solemn agreement to carry out its provisions, by "united force," "if need be." May America always honor and cherish the memory of those brave men! With what astonishment and indignation would they have regarded present-day weakness, selfishness, and cowardice of Americans,—legally citizens, but assuredly not Americans in spirit!

The Compact states:

"That the well being of this country entirely depends, under Divine Providence, on unanimity of sentiment and concurrence in measures, and as clashing interests and opinions, without being under some restraint, will most certainly produce confusion, discord, and almost certain ruin, so we think it our duty to associate and hereby form ourselves into one society for the benefit of present and future settlers, and until the full and proper exercise of the laws of our country can be in use, and the powers of government exerted among us: we do most solemnly and sacredly declare and promise each other that we will faithfully and punctually adhere to, perform and abide by this our Association, and at all times, if need be, compel, by our united force, a due obedience to these, our rules and regulations."

The Cumberland Compact vested authority, for the community's government, in a Court of twelve Judges. These men were to be chosen by the free men of all Stations in the settlement,—that is, all of the small, established gatherings of the pioneers. These were then known as Nashborough (which was to chose three of the Judges), Gasper's and Eaton's (each of which Stations was to elect two of the Judges), Bledsoe's Asher's, Stone's River, Freeland's, and Fort Union (from each of which one Judge was to be sent to the Court).

Fort Nashborough, which was to become Nashville, was the scene of this beginning of civilized government in Tennessee.

ON THE BANKS OF THE BEAUTIFUL WAUTAUGA

The Stately Toast of a More Romantic Age Offered by Landon C. Haynes to East Tennessee

Mr. Chairman and Gentlemen:

"I plead guilty to the soft impeachment! I was born in East Tennessee on the banks of the Wautauga, # which, in the Indian vernacular, is 'Beautiful River,' and beautiful river it is. I have stood upon its banks in my childhood and looked through its glassy waters and have seen a heaven below, and then have looked up and

---

#Here dwelt the early settlers of Tennessee, before Fort Nashborough,—Nashville,—was established.

beheld a heaven above, reflecting like two mirrors, each in the other, its moons and planets and trembling stars,

"Away from its banks of rock and cliff, hemlock and laurel, pine and cedar, stretches back to the distant mountains a vale as beautiful and exquisite as any in Italy or Switzerland. There stands the great Unicoi; the great Black and Smoky Mountains—among the loftiest in the United States of North America—on whose summits the clouds gather of their own accord even on the brightest day.

"There I have seen the Great Spirit of the storm, after noontide, go to take his nap in the pavilion of darkness and of clouds. I have then seen him arise at midnight, as a giant refreshed from slumber, and cover the heavens with gloom and darkness; have seen him awake the tempest, let loose the red lightnings that run along the mountain-tops for a thousand miles, swifter than an eagle's flight in heaven. Then I have seen them stand up and dance, like angels of light in the clouds, to the music of that grand organ of nature, whose keys seemed touched by the fingers of Divinity in the hall of eternity, that responded in notes of thunder, that resounded through the universe.

"Then I have seen the darkness drift away beyond the horizon and the morn get up from her saffron bed, like a queen, put on her robes of light, come forth from her palace in the sun, and stand 'tiptoe on the misty mountain-tops;' and, while night fled from her glorious face to his bed-chamber at the Pole, she lighted the green vale and beautiful river, where I was born and played in my childhood, with a smile of sunshine. O beautiful land of the mountains, with the sun-painted cliffs, how could I ever forget thee?"

THE GREAT SEAL OF THE STATE OF TENNESSEE

"When a Governor of Tennessee, in the full dignity and solemnity of his offices, affixes to official papers his signature and then stamps the paper with the great seal of the State, he is not giving quite so authoritative a stamp to his work as the act seems to imply to his fellow citizens.

"For though since it first entered statehood in 1796, Tennessee has had no less than five great seals, only one of them was ever authorized by the Legislature. And that one is not in use today.

"These five seals, which have been used at various times to lend dignity to state papers, are:

1. The original seal, first used in the Administration of Governor Roane, 1801-1803, which conforms in every respect to the requirements of the report of the Committee adopted by the General Assembly.

2. A different seal, first used in the second series of Administrations of Governor Carroll, 1829-1833.

3. A still different seal, first used in the Administration of Governor Bronlow, 1865-1867.

4. The old seal in the Governor's office, not now used.

5. The great seal in use by the Governor and the Secretary of State at the present time.

"The early pioneers of Tennessee fully appreciated the dignity of the use of official seals. It is not at all unlikely that the Articles of Agreement of the Wautaugua Association (1772) contained a provision requiring the use of a seal, because such provision was made by the Legislature of the State of Franklin (1784-1788); it was intended to have one for the territory of the United States south of the River Ohio (1790-1796), commonly spoken of as the Southwest Territory; and there is a mandatory article in each of the three state constitutions of 1796, of 1834 and of 1870, respectively, requiring the official use of a seal by the Governor.

"The late Colonel W. A. Henderson, in his interesting, but, in some respects, inaccurate paper on the 'Great Seal of the State of Tennessee,' read before the Tennessee Historical Society, in 1894, tells of a message to the Jews, whose authenticity was never doubted, because it 'was written in the name of King Ahasuerus, and Sealed with his Seal.' And, says Colonel Henderson, 'by this most singular device of seals have writing, for centuries, been made to identify the writers.'

"Colonel Henderson continues: 'It will be readily seen, when it is recalled that few who used seals could read or write at all that they had to be individualized with great cunning and kept with great care, so that they could be recognized and might not be wrongfully used. All manner of devices were used, according to the whim of the owner, generally setting forth some dominant personal distinction alleged to himself. It is said that, during the Crusades, the enthusiasts, with common usage, adopted the Holy Cross as their sign manual, thus forever destroying all individuality in the form of a seal.

" 'Again, the greatest care of the owner was to guard his seal. The most trusted officer of Royalty was the "Keeper of the Great Seal." Sometimes a check was held on him by a privy seal, held by the owner, or by another, and the two had to be used together. Or the seal itself was divided into two, three or four sections, like independant locks in a safe, and had to be used in conjunction.

" 'For safety and security, the ordinary seals were usually worn on a finger ring, and were applied to wax much as is done today, except that there was no pretense of an actual sign manual. The Popes of Rome, from unknown origin, used *bullae*, or impressions on metal, much like coin, of iron, brass, silver or gold, as the importance of the document was graded, and it was attached to the writing by a ribbon or thong. These we call Papal Bulls.'

"At its first session, which ended March 31, 1785, the Legislature of the State of Franklin passed 'an act from procuring a great seal for this State.' Concerning this seal, Ramsey says in his Annals of Tennessee:

" 'This act was probably never carried into effect. More than two years afterwards commission to the officers of Franklin were issued, having upon them a common wafer as the seal of the state.'

"A great seal for the territory of the United States of America south of the River Ohio was undoubtedly planned too. In a letter, which General Daniel Smith, secretary of the territory, addressed to Thomas Jefferson, secretary of state, on March 1, 1792, General Smith transmitted a list of the executive acts of Governor Blount from September 1, 1781, to March 1, 1792. His letter further states that a Mr. Allison, a lawyer, who bears the letter, has been designated to employ a person to make a seal for the territory. The letter requested Secretary Jefferson to suggest a proper device for the seal.

"It is indubitable that decision had been made to have a seal for the use of the territorial governor, but there is no evidence that the seal was ever made, for no territorial seal appears on any of Governor Blount's papers.

"In 1796 Tennessee became a state and provisions for a seal were inserted in each of the constitutions which have been formulated since.

"Article II, Section 15, of the constitution of 1796 reads:

" 'There shall be a seal of this state, which shall be kept by the governor, and used by him officially, and shall be called "the Great Seal of the State of Tennessee." '

"Article II, Section 15, of the Constitution of 1834, and Article III, Section 15, of the constitution of 1870, have the identical wording of the section of the constitution of 1796, given above.

"After speaking of the organization of the new state, Colonel Henderson says in his paper:

" 'The first act passed was the incorporation of Blount College, now the University of Tennessee; the second made some military provisions, and the third was the appointment of a committee, consisting of John Sevier, Charles McClung and John Ailer Gammon, for designing and reporting a great seal for the state. From the minds of these men and out of their surroundings was born the seal of our state, and in it was attempted to be crystallized the dominant sentiment of those men and those times.'

"Further on Colonel Henderson says:

" 'On conference of the committee, each member submitted a design for the seal.

" 'Gammon presented the gathering of the clans at Sycamore Shoals, on the Watauga River, preparatory to the march to attack Ferguson, at the moment the draft was taken. This was the only time a military draft was ever resorted to in this state, and it purpose was to allot men who should be compelled to stay at home.

" 'Sevier's design was the blockhouse or "Barracks" at Knoxville, from which a sortie of soldiers was rushing in an attack upon besieging Indians. His remains now sleep on the spot indicated.

" 'McClung's design was finally agreed upon, reported and adopted on the 28th day of March, 1796, and is our seal today.

" 'I have been taught by Dr. Ramsey, the annalist of Tennessee, and first president of this society who knew the committee and most of the actors on that occasion, the reasons that directed that decision, and the ideas that were caught and perpetuated by the typification.'

"It may be well to call attention to the fact that Blount College was established in 1794 by the governor, legislative council and House of Representatives of the territory of the United States south of the River Ohio; that Dr. Ramsey was the fourth president of the Tennessee Historical Society, not the first; and that March 28, 1796 was the first day on which the Legislature convened, after the adoption of the state constitution, on February 6, 1796.

"To continue the quotation from Henderson:

"'After the design presented by Charles McClung had been agreed upon, reported and adopted, the question arose, how could one be prepared? It was needed immediately. It required a kind of work not usual in the settlements, for they had strength of arm rather than cunning of hands. Finally, John Ailor Gammons, deputy clerk of the district court and one of the committee, undertook that task; and his method of procedure was to the last degree primitive. He sawed a cymling half in two, and filled one half with molten lead, and on the flat surface, with a pocket-knife, he rudely fashioned, as best he could, the insignia of the original seal of the state, which was used by Gov. Sevier for some time, until a more pretentious substitute could be fashioned. This quaint relic fell into the hands of Dr. Ramsey, and was preserved by him, intended for this society, together with many other momentoes of Tennessee history, till his dwelling was burned during the war, by an act of vandalism, and all were lost.'

"For the benefit of those who are not familiar with the cymling it may be well to state that the vegetable is a species of summer squash with scalloped edges. Although the 'cymling seal' is not 'our seal today,' as Colonel Henderson asserts it to be, no history of the great seal of the state of Tennessee would be complete without an account of it, especially in view of the vogue which the romantic version has had and the fact that thousands of people firmly believe the story at the present time.

"Such is the simple story of the birth of the first seal, and the interpretation of its rude but pregnant devices, Colonel Henderson continues:

"'It was desired to be shown that she was the sixteenth in the galaxy spanning the political firmament.

"'Next came the insignia of permanent farm life, under which the later-day wisdom (for the two words were not in the original) has added "agriculture." They mean "peace" and "home" and a contented country, in a contra distinction from a hunter's camp or a soldier's foray, while seeking such a place. Rising up from the wilderness, the young state indicated to her children that she gave them the promised land, where the spear should be bent into the pruning-hook and the sword into the ploughshare.

"'Lastly, the "broad-horn," and elaboration of and improvement upon the simple floatboat yet so common upon our rivers meant more than is vaguely understood by the word "commerce." It means a defiance to the King of Spain! Contrary to your blandishments and in spite of your gold, we will remain true to the government we won at King's Mountain and Yorktown...!"

"'These were the ideas dominant in Knoxville on the 28th day of March, 1796, and such is the seal to perpetuate them.'"

That the origin of the Great Seal was the Cymling has been a matter of discussion and has been disputed by Doctor R. L. C. White, who so stated in a paper read before the Tennessee Historical Society on January 9, 1900, although, as above stated, the cymling theory is generally accepted throughout Tennessee. Continuing from the newspaper:

"No official great seal of the State of Tennessee, however, was made until 1802. John Sevier was inaugurated Governor of Tennessee on March 30, 1796. On all his papers on which a seal appears he used his personal seal. So did Governor Roane until April 24, 1802, when the great seal of the State of Tennessee was used for the first time.

"On September 26, 1801, the Senate took the following action: 'On motion of Mr. Taylor, seconded by Mr. Rutledge, a committee was appointed to contract with a suitable person to cut a seal and make a press for this state, and Mr. Taylor and Mr. Rutledge appointed on the part of this house.'

"The committee, however, did not report until November 14, 1801. In the Senate Journal for 1801, is the following entry:

"'Mr. Outlaw from the committee appointed to devise a motto and seal for the state, reported: "The said committee reports that the said seal be a circle, two inches and a quarter in diameter, that the circumference of the circle contain the words, 'THE GREAT SEAL OF TENNESSEE,' that in the lower part of the said circumference be inserted Ferbuary 6, 1796, the date of the constitution of this state: that in the inside of the upper part of the said circle, be set in numerical letters XVI, the number of the state in chronological order; that under the base of the upper semi-circle there be the word, AGRICULTURE; that above the said base, there be the figure of a plough, sheaf of wheat and cotton plant, that in the lower part of the lower semi-circle, there be the word, COMMERCE, and said lower semi-circle, the figure of a boat and boatman."

"The wording in the circumference of the circle was required by the report adopted to be 'The Great Seal of Tennessee.' Yet, when the seal was made, the wording was found to be, 'The Great Seal of the State of Tennessee.' Dr. White noted the discrepancy and said: 'By what authority the extra words were inserted it is impossible now to ascertain, but as they unquestionably improve the dignity of the seal, we need not quarrel with an unknown memory.' Dr. White overlooked the fact that the state constitution required the wording, 'The Great Seal of the State of Tennessee.'

"The Senate Journal, on November 13, 1801, has the following entry:

" 'The committee appointed to contract for sutting a seal for this state and marking a press for said seal.

" 'Report, That they have contracted with William and Mathew Atkinson for the same. . . . . . '

"The Atkinsons did not, however, complete the seal and press and deliver them to the governor until April, 1802. In the archives of the state are official papers of Governor Roane, prior to April 24, 1802, none of which has the great seal of the State of Tennessee affixed to it. But on April 24, 1802, the great seal was used for the first time on the document of which the following is a copy:

" 'Archibald Roane, governor of the State of Tennessee.

" 'To John Maclin, Esquire, treasurer of the Districts of Washington and Hamilton.

" 'Pay to William and Mathew Atkinson one hundred dollars in full compensation for making the great seal of the state, and a press to work the same, agreeably to their contract with the legislature, and this shall be your warrant for so doing.

" 'In testimony whereof, I have hereunto set my hand and caused the great seal of the state to be affixed at Knoxville, this 24th day of April, 1802, Archibald Roane.

Tennessee Flag

" 'By the Governor. Wm. Maclin, Secretary.'

"Not only was the great seal of Tennessee made by the Atkinsons, used by Governor Roane, but it was used by every successive governor down to and including Governor Hall, as shown by official documents in the state archives. After 1829, however, in the second series of Governor Carroll's administrations, a different seal was used. By whose authority the new seal was made there are no records to show.

"In 1915 Hallam W. Goodloe, formerly Secretary of State of Tennessee and, at that time, private secretary to Gov. Tom C. Rye, placed on the wall of the governor's outer office a framed article on the Great Seal of the State of Tennessee, which had been published June 25, 1910, in the ninety-eighth anniversary edition of the Nashville American. Over the seal, Mr. Goodloe placed a framed memorandum which reads as follows:

" 'The Great Seal of the State of Tennessee, described in this framed article, was placed in the governor's office by Governor Rye in 1915 after it was discarded and its stone base removed from the secretary of state's office, "to make more room." '

"The seal used by Carroll in 1833 was only one and three-fourths inches wide; the date February 6 is omitted, and the boat is entirely different from the original and is pointed in the opposite direction. There are differences, too, in the details of execution of the engraving, not only of the boat but also of the plow, the sheaf of wheat and the stalk of cotton.

"The same changed seal was used by the successive governors until the administration of Brownlow, when some of the papers contain the seal first used by Carroll, and other papers contain still another seal, nearly as wide as the original seal, being a fraction more than two inches width. On this third seal also the boat points in the same direction as that of the original seal and yet is very similar to that first used by Carroll. The new Brownlow seal appears on the bonds under Brownlow in 1868, also on those issued under Governor Senter in 1869 and on those issued under Gov. John C. Brown in 1873.

"The old seal in the governor's office differs from the seal now in use in size, being only two inches in diameter, and in slight details concerning engraved parts."

The foregoing quotations are excerpts from two articles, by A. P. Foster, in *The Nashville Tennessean Magazine*, Nashville, Tennessee, July 7, 1935, and July 14, 1935. They are presented herein by the kind permission of *The Nashville Tennessean Magazine*.

The Volunteer State

"Tennessee is known as the 'Volunteer State' because of the manner in which its citizens rallied around Andrew Jackson in the War of 1812. Not only so, but in every war thousands of Tennesseans have eagerly enlisted, not waiting to be drafted."

The State Flower of Tennessee
The Iris

The floral emblem of the State of Tennessee is the Iris. The Legislature recorded its views formally regarding the Tennessee State Flower and the fact of that flower's adoption is duly recorded in the archives of the state.

Tennessee State-Song

O Tennessee, that gave us birth, to thee our hearts bow down,
For thee our love and loyalty shall weave a fadeless crown.
Thy purple hills our cradle was, they fields our mother's breast,
Beneath thy sunny blended skies our childhood days were blessed.

Chorus

O Tennessee, fair Tennessee, our love for thee
  Can never die, dear Tennessee!

'Twas long ago our fathers came, a free and noble band,
Across the mountains' frowning heights to seek a promised land,
And here, before their raptured eyes in beauteous majesty,
Outspread the smiling valleys of the winding Tennessee.

Could we forget our heritage of heroes strong and brave?
Could we do aught but cherish it unsullied to the grave?
Ah, no! the State where Jackson sleeps shall ever peerless be.
We glory in thy majesty, our homeland, Tennessee!

The words of this song are by Nell Grayson Taylor, and the music by Roy Lamont Smith. It was adopted as a State-song by the legislature of Tennessee, in 1925. In 1931, the legislature also adopted as another State-song, "My Tennessee," words and music by Frances Hannah Tranum.

Nashville's First Postmaster

A few years ago a bronze tablet was erected to honor Nashville's first Postmaster, Captain John Gordon, and contains the following inscription:

"Captain John Gordon—1763-1819—First Postmaster of Nashville, 1796, 1797. Born in Virginia. Came to Nashville in 1782, became noted defender against the Indians of old Fort Nashboro and the frontier settlements. Captain of a spy company of the Davidson County Regiment, participated in the Nickajack expedition which ended Indian atrocities on the Cumberland. As Captain of the spies, reporting only to General Jackson, he distinguished himself in every battle of Jackson's Creek campaign. In 1814 he performed alone a mission of great danger, as Jackson's special envoy to the Spanish Governor of Pensacola, resulting in the capture of Pensacola, and the cession of Florida to the United States. He led his company during the Seminole War of 1817-18. Buried at Columbia, Tennessee.

"Erected 1932 by the Division of History of the State of Tennessee and the Descendants of John Gordon."

The above article concerning the first Postmaster of Nashville, Tennessee, will be of interest as William Dean McNish, father of Nellie Louise (McNish) Gambill, was the Civil War Postmaster of this office. Biographical account of William Dean McNish and his family have been given in Part II of the present work.

The Author's Epilogue

These chronicles represent hours of research and while some of the family-lines may not be complete, I hope they will serve as stepping-stones to further knowledge for those interested in tracing their ancestry. Realizing that there are many other records I should like to have included in this book, it is with regret I close its pages and write the word,

FINISH

NELL McNISH GAMBILL

APPENDIX

BIRTHS

	PAGE
Theodore Charles Knecht, born Tuesday morning at ten forty-five o'clock, April 30, 1940. Son of Ted C. and Julia Huggins Knecht	123
Elizabeth Candace Love, daughter of Lieutenant-Colonel Robert Worrell and Cornelia Gambill Love, born in the Canal Zone, June 2, 1941	121
Robert Wheless Love, son of Lieutenant-Colonel Robert Worrell and Cornelia Gambill Love, born August 25, 1944 in Nashville, Tennessee	121
William Glasgow Gambill, son of Benjamin Drake Smith and Mary Bell Glasgow Gambill, born May 4, 1942	123
Benjamin Drake Smith Gambill, Junior, son of Benjamin Drake Smith and Mary Bell Glasgow Gambill, born February 28, 1945	123
Linda Kathleen Cox, born November 7, 1945, daughter of Albert and Margaret Laney Cox	176
Barbara Jane Banks, born November 6, 1943, daughter of Edwin McKinney and Jane Randolph Bush Banks	177
Winfield Scott Cloyd, born September 15, 1944, in Chicago, Illinois	159
Thomas Mitchell Mann McNish, born May 1, 1942, son of Edgar Mann and Elenora Kinsey McNish	150
Clare Whittington, born September 29, 1944, daughter of Lieutenant-Colonel and Martha Farrell Whittington, Dallas, Texas	119
David Carsey Blood, born August 29, 1944, son of William and Evelyn Carsey Blood	138
William Quinton Dunbar, son of William Matheson and Marie Smith Dunbar	176

MARRIAGES

	PAGE
James T. (Zeke) Carsey, married Helen Fischer of New York City	138
Dorothy Matthews, to Charles Foulds, Detroit, Michigan	159
Mary Elenora Kinsey, to Edgar Mann McNish, May 27, 1939	150
Kathleen Stump, to John Hunter Matthews, May 6, 1940	159
Edwin McKinney Banks, born May 14, 1912, married Jane Bush, October 31, 1936, Charlotte, North Carolina	177
Margaret Locke Laney, married Albert Warren Cox, January 23, 1945, Charlotte, North Carolina	176
Martha Farrell, to Captain Robert Gaston Whittington, Junior, 16th October, 1943, Dallas, Texas	119
Bonnie Hager, to Lieutenant Raymond Daume, April 2, 1945	153
Captain David Kelly McNish, II, married Val Sturtridge of Brisbane, Australia. Have one son, David, III	150
Betty Matthews to Monroe Daniel Stroeker, November 27, 1941	161
Ruth Matthews to Fred J. Ringel, June 4, 1940, Detroit, Michigan	159
Marie Smith, married William Matheson Dunbar, May 6, 1939	176

DEATHS

	PAGE
Mrs. Elizabeth Stewart Scruggs, died February 26, 1941	96
Mrs. Elizabeth H. Armistead, died January 13, 1941	77
Beckham Lee Douglass, resident of Denver 52 years, died November 7, 1944	175
Hugh Lawson McNish, Junior, died February 12, 1940	153
Mrs. Lemira H. Fall, died April 8, 1942	104
Mrs. Maggie Lee Smith Briggs, died March 31, 1933, Charlotte, North Carolina	176
James Criddle Hinton, died May 30, 1932, Nashville, Tennessee	104
William Wheless Gambill, Junior, died June 6, 1945	120
Mary Louis Laney, died February 4, 1937	176
Dean McNish, died April 8, 1943	147
Robert C. Kenyon, died June, 1944	139

www.ingramcontent.com/pod-product-compliance
Lightning Source LLC
Chambersburg PA
CBHW070536170426
43200CB00011B/2439